When God Says No

When God Says No

*The Mystery of Suffering
and the Dynamics of Prayer*

∾

Daniel Lanahan, O.F.M.

Lantern Books • New York
A Division of Booklight Inc.

2001
Lantern Books
One Union Square West, Suite 201
New York, NY 10003

Printed in the United States of America

Library of Congress Cataloging-in-Publication Data

ɪan, Daniel.
When God says no : the mystery of suffering and the
dynamics of prayer / Daniel Lanahan.
        p. cm.
Includes bibliographical references.
ISBN 1-930051-90-5 (pbk.)
        1. Suffering—Religious aspects—Christianity. 2. Prayer. I.
Title.

BV4909 .L36 2001
248.8'6—dc21

                                                    2001038434

To Neil Lanahan (1929–1974)
my brother and mentor
in the school of suffering,
with the hope that this book
is a partial answer to his prayer
that "great good" will come from his illness.

Table of Contents

Acknowledgments

MANY PERSONS, MORE than I can name, helped me in the writing of this book. Some, however, should be named:

I thank first of all my Franciscan community at Ho-Ho-Kus, New Jersey, who enabled me to take a sabbatical to write this book. Thanks to my sisters Peggy and Maureen (a.k.a. Sr. Jean Aquinas, O.P. and Sr. Genevieve, L.S.P.) for painfully recalling their memories of the events surrounding Neil's last six months.

Thanks to my confrere, Fr. Gabriel Scarfia, O.F.M. for critically reading the manuscript and for making several worthwhile suggestions concerning the theology underlying my thoughts. His encouragement convinced me to publish.

A huge thanks to my friend, Sr. Cindy Matthews, O.S.F. who has been urging me for years to write this book. She also donated her time, talent, and treasury of rich insights and practical wisdom that helped greatly to move the text from being a purely theological treatise to a more pastoral presentation.

For all those who previewed the manuscript for clarity and comprehensibility, I am most grateful.

Finally, I thank Gene Gollogly, my publisher, for his enthusiastic encouragement. For Carol Dunn's editing skills, I will be forever grateful.

❧ Introduction

IN THE GARDEN of Gethsemane Jesus prayed that the "cup be taken from him" if it be God's will. God answered no.

Three times St. Paul begged God to remove the "thorn from his side." Three times God said no.

When my family prayed desperately for my brother Neil to be cured of melanoma, God said no. When we prayed for a twenty-five-year-old niece to survive a car accident, God said no. When the people of the Holocaust prayed, when the victims of war in the former Yugoslavia, or in any of the hundred places war is being waged at any given time prayed; when people afflicted with cancer, alcoholism, or AIDS prayed for deliverance; when the victims of physical, sexual, or emotional abuse prayed to be spared, the answer was no.

During the past fifteen years of preaching parish missions, I have constantly been challenged to minister effectively to people struggling with their faith in a God who answered their prayers with a no. Almost always, these people brought up the promise of Jesus: If you ask anything of God in my name, it will be given to you. Ask and you shall receive. How could Jesus teach and expect us to believe what every Christian knows to be literally untrue?

This book is not another theological or philosophical attempt to provide a rational solution to the divine puzzle of why God allows innocent people to suffer or why our prayers in Jesus' name are not effective. This book attempts to provide simple, practical, pastoral insights for the ordinary person who comes to listen to the Word of God when we assemble as Church. To maintain this focus, each chapter begins with a letter from Ellen, a believer searching for wisdom.

Chapter One reflects on the dynamics of prayer, especially the distinction between prayer and the prayer of petition. I include the place of prayer in the life of Jesus as well as his teaching regarding the prayer of petition. I examine our own personal encounter with God in prayer before concluding with a look at how my brother Neil's prayers were or were not answered.

The second chapter touches upon the mystery of suffering in its relationship to the reality of creation, especially in the light of a new cosmology (our systematic understanding of the universe). Our image of a benign, elderly man with a long beard enthroned above the stars who looks down lovingly on this world must give way to a God who is "Incomprehensible Mystery yet everywhere obvious" (Karl Rahner). God is the reality that energizes an infinitely expanding universe. This God does not ordinarily say no to the nature and laws of creation. God does not ordinarily suspend the laws of gravity to prevent a falling object from landing upon its victim. Yet, God is everywhere present as Mystery, and miracles of all kinds happen.

The middle two chapters deal with the central event of all history—namely, the birth, death, and resurrection of Jesus. Why did Jesus choose to make himself poor by accepting the human condition? Why did Jesus say to Nicodemus "the Son of Man must be lifted up" (on the cross)? Why did Jesus have to die on the cross to save us? What precisely did Jesus save us from? Finally, what did Jesus save us *for*? How do we participate in the mystery of Jesus who came not to take away suffering, or to explain it away, but to fill it with his presence?

My brother Neil's suffering and death have been the heaviest sorrows of my life. Even after twenty-five years, if I allow myself to remember his last days, a deep pain wells up within me and suddenly, like flood waters, it overflows to wipe me out. For that reason, this book has not been an easy one to write. It was conceived in pain and delivered with tears. You may, perhaps, sense the salt on some pages! Yet, my brother's presence in my life has not ended, only changed. Chapter Five details some of the profound ways Neil touched upon my life and ministry.

When God Says No ends in Heaven. Face to face with God, we will not be given the answer to the question that no theology, no book, not even the Bible, no dogma, no authority, not even that of the Church, has ever answered: Why the suffering of the innocent? Instead, we will be blessed with the fullness of salvation and healing and made whole at last. We will be with the Answer in love forever.

☙

1: Prayers and Prayers of Petition

Dear Dan,

Would you please explain how Jesus could possibly urge us to ask anything in His name and the Father will grant it, when almost everyone who does ask for a cure does not receive what they asked for? God said no to my prayer when my father was dying of pancreatic cancer. Was my faith too weak, were my sins so great? Do maybe our prayers help us to get through hard times and not affect God in any way? Do you believe that our prayers can move God to change things in our world?

Waiting patiently, your friend
Ellen

ELLEN IS NOT only my friend, but my biggest
agitator. What she challenges, however, needs to be
challenged. My response is going to disappoint her,
because there isn't a simple explanation for her
profound question. As the revelation of who God is,
did Jesus give her false hope? God loves you, ask
anything, it will gladly be given to you. How can we
reconcile our Lord's emphasis on our loving
relationship to the Father/Abba with the clear
evidence that Abba does not always answer our
prayers with a yes. We understand when our prayer
to win the lottery isn't answered affirmatively; but,
when it involves the serious illness of a loved one, we
wonder about this God Who is Love.

To begin, Ellen, I do not comprehend God. The
more I study and reflect and pray, the more incomprehensible God becomes to me. When I was a
student studying for a degree in theology, I actually
spoke as if I knew a lot about God and the ways of the
Divine. Maybe I *did* know a lot about God, but today
I am more aware of being an "agnostic." The Holy
Unknowable is my God; I believe firmly in the unfathomable mystery of God.

The God of Genesis dwelling above the bowl of
the sky has given way to the God of an infinitely
expanding universe, to a God who is, in the terms

used by the theologian Karl Rahner that I mentioned in the Introduction, "the Incomprehensible Mystery yet everywhere obvious"—at least, to those who sense the presence of the Divine. I believe that this God is a loving, friendly God who knew me in my mother's womb. Having said all that, you will readily appreciate that all my attempts at explaining when God says no end up as at best the utterances of an infant!

First, we must be open to all that God has revealed about prayer in the Scriptures and not focus on one or two lines. Scripture explains Scripture. To take our Lord's words literally without qualifications will lead to grave disappointment.

Again I tell you, if two of you join your voices on earth to pray for anything whatever, it shall be granted to you by my Father in heaven. (Matt. 18:19–20)

Ask, and you will receive. Seek, and you will find. Knock and it shall be opened to you. For the one who asks, receives. The one who seeks, finds. The one who knocks, enters. Would one of you hand his son a stone when he asks for a loaf, or a poisonous snake when he asks for a fish? If you, with all your sins, know how to give your children what is good, how

*much more will your heavenly Father give good
things to anyone who asks him!* (Matt. 7:7–11)

If these statements of Jesus in the Gospels are taken
literally, without qualifications, they are manifestly
untrue. Times without number people have prayed
passionately alone or with a whole nation for deliverance from war, a plague, an egocentric tyrant, from
the Holocaust—and their prayers were not, in the
literal sense, ever answered, or the answers seemed to
have been no.

In my particular case, we had the Franciscans,
Dominicans, the Little Sisters of the Poor, and
hundreds of relatives and friends praying for my
brother, Neil, to survive melanoma. Six months later
he was dead. There is no point in refusing to face the
facts of the situation, and nothing but harm can result
from teaching people to expect what does not happen.

Furthermore, I learned that my being a priest and
a Franciscan, and my sisters also religious in the
service of the Most High, did not entitle us to an
advantage over any of God's children. Yes, I confess to
reminding God of the petition of His "humble servant
and handmaids." Once I even tried to take advantage
of being a priest—surely, God will hear the prayer of
this priest. Little did I realize at the time how I had
tried to put God in the position of showing

preference. In my desire to save my brother from terrible pain, I desperately tried every possible angle, even asking God to exempt me and mine from the ordinary course of the human condition.

A second disquieting aspect of my being a priest flowed from my belief that I possessed the gift of healing. Several times in my priestly ministry I have prayed with or over people who subsequently claimed a cure from a definitely diagnosed ailment. During Neil's illness, I thought God would surely hear me and use me in curing my own brother of cancer. When Neil was not cured, I stopped believing I had the gift, until other instances took place. Certainly some people, like Fr. Ralph DiOrio and Sr. Briege McKenna, have the gift to a larger extent, yet I had doubts about myself. Why is the gift not always operative? Why did I fail to be an instrument for my brother? When I realized later that the prayer of the Great High Priest and Healer of the world in Gethsemane did not deliver the Son of Man from suffering, I was less upset!

Does God Say No Because of Our Weak Faith or Our Sins?

To address Ellen's question about prayer not being answered because of a lack of faith and/or because of past sins, I have two brief replies:

First, Jesus taught that, even if our faith is as small as a mustard seed, we could say to this mountain, move from here to there, and it would move (Matt. 17:20). Jesus assures us that, even when our faith is small and weak, God can still help us to do the impossible. We should not blame ourselves when our prayer fails to be answered as we would like. Nor should we presume that our faith is all it should be. Like the apostles, we always need to pray: Increase our faith.

Perhaps it is not a question of a lack of faith, but a lack of confidence. There is a lovely woman in Holy Cross parish in Springfield, Massachusetts who has absolute confidence that God or the angels will provide a parking space for her whenever she needs one in busy, downtown Springfield. She always finds one. We can chalk this up to coincidence, but have you noticed that coincidences happen more when we pray? My point is this: How aware are we of the many times God has answered our many petitions? Do we lack confidence because we do not recognize God's answers? Have we allowed our prayer's failure to cure our loved one to undermine our basic faith in a God who cares?

Secondly, our sins can prevent God from answering some of our prayers—e.g. how can God bring peace to a person who continues to be unforgiving towards others? (I am not saying that we should forgive and forget. Often our memories are necessary for our growth.) If we close ourselves to grace, how can God give us blessings? However, God does not reject the sinner, only the sin. Our sins do not prevent God from answering some of our prayers. If we pray for another's health and well-being, our heart is open. It may be open only a little, but it is open to God's grace and blessings. To pray for the cure of another is a graceful act and does not prevent God from acting, if God so wills it.

Prayer and Prayers of Petition

Before going further into our Lord's words regarding our prayers being answered, we absolutely need to situate the prayer of petition in its relationship to the whole subject of prayer. The English word prayer comes from the Latin verb *precari*, which means to beg, ask, or entreat. The one we ask or entreat is usually God, before whom we always stand, at least implicitly, in need, since we are not God. Prayer includes, in its widest sense, every communion with God, whether in a petition or in any other way.

The Heart of Prayer

The essence of prayer is carrying on a personal relationship with God. This relationship has often been described in terms of an "I–Thou" encounter. We address God as a "Thou," someone we speak to in a dialogue directly and not as a third person bystander.

This is true, but I prefer the language used by Beatrice Bruteau in *Radical Optimism*, where the author emphasizes our radical union with God by virtue of our baptism. God lives in us, and we live in God. So, when we pray, it is not an "I–Thou" but an "I–I" relationship. The Spirit prays in us and we pray in the Spirit. God lives and moves in us and we live and move in God. This understanding of our life of grace immediately situates the reality of prayer and, in particular, our petitions, in the context of our very special personal relationship with God.

How often are we mindful of the fact that our prayers (in particular, our petitions) are actions of someone connected intimately with God? Our prayers are, first and foremost, expressions of an intimacy with the Intimate. The God who chose us in Christ initiated this relationship out of love, and rejoices whenever one heart speaks to the Other.

Invaluable insights about prayer come from looking at the habits of Jesus concerning prayer. He taught by word and example that prayer is necessary for salvation. Though he was the incarnate Son of God, he frequently prayed; it is remarkable how many times the New Testament makes mention of Jesus and prayer. Prayer was a way of life to Jesus, an integral part of his life. Not only did he spend nights in prayer, especially before some significant event (choosing the twelve apostles, his passion and death), but his whole life was replete with occasions where his prayers expressed thanksgiving, praise, petition, and trust.

Jesus revealed his deepest self in his prayers. He was, before all else, the Son of the Father, Abba. His prayers revealed that he came to do the Father's will, completely trusting God and resolutely committed to fulfill the mission given to him. He was one with the Father in thought, purpose, and affection. Jesus was the revelation, the embodiment of God's love for us, and one with God in working for our salvation.

Jesus was, first and foremost, a person of prayer. His prayer life flowed out of his deepest self as the incarnate Son of God. Does our prayer life flow out of our deepest awareness of ourselves as beloved sons and daughters of a God who cares?

Personally, my own prayer life developed gradually from understanding prayer as saying prayers to a situation where prayer was a personal encounter with God in faith and love. Obviously, my prayer life flowed out of my spiritual life. My under-standing of my relationship to God prior to my ordination in 1962 reflected a theology of grace that viewed grace as a "thing" — not a material thing, but as an external help to enable me to do good and avoid evil. In those years, most of us did not understand grace in terms of an interpersonal relationship with God.

In the Fall of 1962, the Second Vatican Council opened and my life with God likewise opened to new dimensions. While pursuing a graduate degree in theology at Catholic University in Washington, DC, God sent a special grace to me embodied in the person of a fellow graduate student. One day, after a fascinating presentation on the spirituality of St. John of the Cross by another embodiment of God's grace, Fr. Ernest Larkin, a Carmelite, I stayed in the classroom as people emptied out. My whole inner being was awakened, excited as my mind started to connect what I had just heard from Fr. Larkin to many aspects of the spiritual life.

I can't describe the joy I felt as a kind of chain reaction started to happen within me. That day I learned for the first time that not only does God desire that we live a good life in service to others, but that God wants to have a relationship with us that is intimate—similar to the interpersonal intimacy that friends have with one another or spouses with each other. I was having this unusual moving moment of insight, when God's embodiment of grace in the person, of all things, a Jesuit (a bit of God's humor) started to speak. It was an extraordinary and unique experience, because this man's first words actually completed the sentence I was thinking at that moment!

In the course of our graduate year together, I experienced the intimacy of friendship for the first time. Of course, there were many wonderful, loving, and caring people already in my life, but this was the first time I lowered my ego-boundaries to allow someone to come inside to experience my vulnerable self with my fears, anxieties, etc. Through a gradual build-up of trust, I was set free to invite someone into my inner sanctum. Through this experience of intimacy, I started to realize the kind of relationship God desires to have with us. It would be wonderful to relate that I immediately "fell head over heels" in love with God and my life ever since has been one continuously deepening love affair. However, what I can state, happily, is that my whole concept of the spiritual life of grace radically altered. Specifically, prayer became life with the living God expressed at given times in prayers of thanksgiving, praise, adoration, and petition.

Keeping in mind prayer as a personal encounter with God in faith and love, we can now return to the question of the effectiveness of our prayers of petition.

Can Our Prayer Move God to Affect Change in Our World?

There is an old saying that God always answers our prayers, but sometimes the answer is yes, sometimes no, and sometimes wait.

Once upon a time a child was talking to God.

"What is a million dollars like to you?" the child asked God.

God answered: "A million dollars is like a penny to me."

The child then asked: "What is a million years like to you?"

"A million years is like a second to me," God replied.

Finally, the child boldly begged: "Could I have one of your pennies?"

"Yes," God quickly responded, "but could you wait a second?"

What the child learned, we too must accept—namely, that we cannot trick God into granting our petitions. While our prayers cannot change God, the good news is that God's attitude towards us does not need to be changed. God is Love, and our salvation and happiness are the will of God. The good news is even better. God listens to our entreaties and, when it is for our salvation, God can be moved to enter into a situation through the persons involved. Some theologians and many philosophers would have problems with this position, but experiences of God's action in response to prayer affirm the position.

Let us choose an uncomplicated example taken from the area of the pastoral ministry that involves helping someone who is grieving.

Jean's mother passes away and is buried in her Vermont hometown. When Jean is driving back to her home in Springfield, Massachusetts, she prays that God will send her a sign that her mother is at peace in Heaven. She prays to receive her mother's favorite flower, a yellow rose.

Meanwhile, back in Springfield, Sr. Cindy, the pastoral minister in Jean's parish, is busy visiting the sick and handling routine tasks of the day. Several times in the course of the day, Sr. Cindy receives an impulse to go to the florist to pick up a yellow rose for Jean and leave it at her back door. Initially, she decides not to buy the rose; she reasons that she does not really know Jean that well, and she does not want to be too forward. Each time the thought returns it becomes more annoying and Cindy wonders why she cannot simply stick with the decision she has made, why the thought keeps hounding her. As the workday draws to a close, the nagging idea comes once more.

Finally, she decides she will give in to this persistent urging before she drives home across town and has to drive back again just to drop off the yellow rose!

Late at night, with a very heavy heart, Jean arrives home with her husband. When she opens the screen door, she lets out a scream and starts crying as she picks up her sign from God, a yellow rose. While God ordinarily does not deliver roses, God can and does operate directly within people (Cindy) to answer a prayer (Jean's).

Once, when returning to Buffalo from a trip to New York City, I discovered to my chagrin at the airport parking lot that my car's battery was dead. I had failed to shut off the headlights when I exited the car early that foggy morning. This was in the days before cell phones, so I walked out of the parking lot and across the main highway to the nearest service station for help. Unfortunately, the attendant was alone and could not leave the station. He called a service station nearby only to learn that there was no one who could jump-start my car. At this point, I called home, Christ the King Seminary, and one of the professors agreed to come right out. He told me he would be there in twenty minutes.

While I waited, I calmly said to myself: This is so strange; it is the first time I forgot to shut the car lights off resulting in a dead battery. Here I am, stuck at the gas station on Genesee Street for twenty or thirty minutes. Then the thought came to me: Am I supposed to be here for some reason? Just then the attendant said: "This is strange, not one car has come into the station in over ten minutes." When he said "This is strange," I realized that I had used the same words in my thoughts. So, I immediately began to engage the young man in conversation.

To make a long story short, the young man had run away from home before graduating from high school, and was now "lost" in Buffalo, experiencing hard times financially and emotionally. By chance (?), I knew his parents from my years at St. Bonaventure University, although I had never met this young man. He was open to my advice to return home, to reconsider his options, and to try again to venture forth. Throughout my time with him, I felt the presence of grace. God does not jump-start dead batteries; God can and does operate directly within people (me) to answer an unspoken prayer (the young man's) or his parents' prayer for his return home.

While these moments of grace in answer to prayers are significant, the more important question is: Are we people of prayer who reflect upon our experiences to detect the hand of the Creator in the events of our life? How many times has God been moved by our prayers? We will never know unless we choose silence and search for the incomprehensible yet everywhere obvious God through a life of prayer.

God's No to Jesus

All genuine prayer strengthens our relationship with God, and, therefore, is always effective and always heard. When we pray for ourselves or a loved one to be delivered from some painful suffering, we must keep in mind that it is our relationship with God that sustains us, delivers us, and enables us to accept the situation.

The best example of this in the New Testament is Jesus himself. In the Garden of Gethsemane, Jesus prayed in terror that the cup might pass from him and that he might be delivered from the agonizing situation facing him. God said no and Jesus said yes. In saying yes, Jesus surrendered his life into the hands of his Father and accepted the Cross as the Father's way to the glory of his resurrection and the salvation of the whole world. It did not make Jesus' journey through the Cross to the Resurrection any less painful ("Father, why have you abandoned me?"). It changed his way of looking at the situation and he was enabled to bear the unbearable.

God's No to St. Paul

You may recall how St. Paul three times prayed that he might be delivered from the thorn in the flesh. He was not delivered from that situation, he was asked to accept it; and in that very situation he discovered the strength that was made perfect in his weakness and the grace which is sufficient for all things. In that strength and grace the situation was not only accepted, but also transformed into glory.

> *In order that I might not become conceited I was given a thorn in the flesh, as an angel of Satan to beat me and keep me from getting proud. Three times I begged the Lord that this might leave me. He said to me, "My grace is enough for you, for in weakness power reaches perfection." And so I willingly boast of my weaknesses instead, that the power of Christ may rest upon me.* (2 Cor. 12:7–10)

Personally, the closest experience to Paul's and our Lord's situation that I ever had involved a painful year-long "crucifixion" as a victim of political intrigue in higher education. People circumvented the proper channels and eventually were able to force me to resign the presidency of a graduate school. Many, many times I prayed to be delivered from the excruciating ordeal of being caught in a power play. I was not delivered from that situation; I was asked to accept it; and, in going through it, I discovered that God's grace was sufficient for me. The dark night of pain and apparent defeat, eventually, after three years (not three days) turned into a wonderful resurrection experience, where my faith in God and the reality of the death and resurrection of the Lord in our lives were confirmed. Now, I thank God for the suffering (caused by human beings, not given by God) that brought me such freedom and peace and joy.

As we can appreciate, God does not ordinarily deliver us from difficult situations, but enables us to come through them—not as victims or survivors, but as victors.

Neil's Prayers of Petition

Several days after the cancer surgery that necessitated the amputation of his left leg, my brother Neil penned the following letter:

> *To Whom It May Concern —*
>
> *My illness gives pause to all—and what has sustained me needs be told for all to hear—For it would be tragic indeed if no good comes of my illness—I hope great good comes of my illness.*
>
> *I was chiefly sustained during the period before the operation by my abiding faith in God and His*

Son and that all works according to their plans. I asked the Living God in the name of the Son to bring me through the operation – "Ask and you shall receive." I asked Jesus in the name of his Mother for the same favor – For formalistic prayers I relied on the Hail Mary *– without which I do not think I would have gotten through the operation.*

On a natural level – I found strength in one simple thing – that I never in my life deliberately tried to hurt anyone's feelings – that I tried to above all else assure that my mother's feelings were secure – that she would not be abandoned.

So in the last analysis, it was love of God, love of Mother that sustained me – and I would think others could find strength in these things also.

I want to thank everyone for all their prayers – and especially my family for their help.

I am sorry for causing all this trouble – Love,

Neil

Neil's trust in God and his love for the Mother of God and the Rosary enabled him to bear the unbearable. I am witness to his faith. His spirit triumphed over the cancer even though it appeared the cancer won. My hope is that Neil heard from the Father at the moment of his death the beautiful, comforting, deeply moving words of the Song of Songs:

> *Come, my love, the winter is past*
> *Come, I long to see your face.*

Did God Say No to Neil?

If someone looked merely at the surface of the events of my brother's suffering and death, that person would come to the quick conclusion: Neil received a no to his prayers for a cure. Yet, when we take a closer look, we begin to realize that God answered his prayer with a resounding yes!

Neil prayed for God to help him through the ordeal of the operation. The night before the operation, an orderly came to prep Neil for what Neil had thought was going to be surgery on the calf of his left leg where the cancerous mole was. When the orderly informed Neil that the doctor had ordered the entire leg up to the hip to be prepped, Neil's whole being shook with terrible fright.

When I walked into the room after the prepping, I immediately saw a different Neil. He was terrified and almost beside himself. He was experiencing his Agony in the Garden, and, like Jesus, he needed to be alone. He said that I needed to go home. He told me later, and it is also contained in his letter, that the only way he got through the hours after the prepping until he fell asleep was the prayerful reciting of the Hail Mary. His terrified mind could not concentrate on anything, except the familiar words of the Hail Mary.

As Neil's letter testified, he was sustained "by his abiding faith in God and His Son and that all works according to their plans." He asked the Living God in the name of the Son to bring him through the operation. God answered Neil's prayer; God did say no to the miraculous curing of the cancer, but God said yes to sustaining Neil through the operation. His letter written after the operation clearly indicates that God said yes to his prayers.

God said yes to another important prayer of Neil's—namely, that our mother would not feel abandoned. When Neil was in his last days on earth, he reminded me that our mother had a great fear of being abandoned, a fear that came from being left by her widowed mother with relatives in Ireland when she was three years old. Her mother went to the United States to seek employment and one day to bring her child to this country. Neil made me promise, above all else, to assure our mother that she was secure, that she would never be abandoned. Like Jesus handing his mother over to the beloved disciple, John, Neil entrusted our mother into my care. For the remaining twenty years of her life, she was never left alone for more than an hour at any given time.

Through my wonderful sister, Peggy, a Dominican Sister of Amityville, New York, some great friends, as well as live-in help, my mother was able to stay secure in her own home for many years until she needed skilled care. Then, my sister Maureen, a Little Sister of the Poor, and her community provided not only a safe haven but added years to her life by their tender, loving care. God said no to my brother's prayer that he might survive to take care of his mother, but God said yes to his prayer by sending an army of people to assure her that she was not abandoned. May Neil rest in the peace that his prayers were answered. God did say yes.

∽

🐝 2: The Mystery of Suffering

Dear Dan,

Peace! Your explanation of our Lord's teaching on prayer, in particular your advice not to focus on one or two sentences but to see prayer in the light of other passages in the New Testament, especially Jesus's prayer in the Garden of Gethsemane, has helped me to realize that my own prayers are mostly prayers based on the last words of the Our Father: Deliver us from all evil. Can't tell you that you answered all my questions about my apparently ineffective prayers for loved ones who are gravely ill. Would you please address the question behind all

the other questions: How can a loving God allow,
not cause, innocent people to suffer?

Your loving good-friend,
Ellen

EVEN THOUGH YOU gave me at most a B+ for an obviously A+ reflection on prayer, I will bury my hurt and move into the hardest question in the world! You phrased it well. One Holocaust survivor expressed it by way of conclusion: How can anyone continue to believe in a benevolent God after Auschwitz?

Ellen, while I openly profess that I do not know the answer to your crucial question, you know that I think I have some answers to some parts of your question. These partial answers have value for me and derive from my experience as a believer who has found believing a painful journey at times.

To begin to address your question, we need to start and end with a word that has unfortunately almost disappeared from the vocabulary and thinking of people today. That word is "mystery."

Life is full of mysteries. I don't mean of the whodunnit variety, but in the sense of realities we have only begun to understand. Who of us claims to know the workings of the human heart in all its dimensions or the nature and extent of the physical universe, to name two subjects? In theology, we reflect upon many mysteries: God, the Trinity, Grace, Eternal Life, and many more. These mysteries can only be known in part; we will never comprehend them in this life. One of *the* mysteries that should carry a "product-warning" label is the mystery of suffering and death—specifically, when bad things happen to innocent people.

How many believers have stopped practicing their religion when a terrible personal tragedy has struck— e.g. the death from cancer of a three-year-old daughter or son? How many people lost faith in God during the twentieth century, which will go down in infamy for its violence and culture of death? Some of the major spokespersons of the Holocaust gave up on God (if God was absent to them then, they will be absent to God now).

Real mystery demands real humility. There are many brilliant people who have given up on God because they could not comprehend how a loving God could allow such horrible injustices to take place. Because they could not comprehend the action or non-action of such a God, they rejected God. We all need to acknowledge that a God we could comprehend would be a God we would eventually have to reject. Our finite minds cannot completely grasp the reality of God and God's ways. To set out to understand completely the mystery of suffering, especially in innocent lives, is not only impossible, but dangerous. My point is this: We need to be humble as we start to explore the many aspects of this mystery, and not to reject God because we cannot fully understand how an infinitely good and all-powerful God allows people to suffer.

Christianity does not really have anything comparable to the prayers of Lamentations in the Hebrew Scriptures. The Book of Job is essentially a lamentation about the misfortunes of life, and Job and his friends attempt to make sense of them in the light of their faith in the God of the Covenant. I believe our anguish, our persistence in seeking some explanation of why God allows people to suffer, approaches the nature of a lamentation. In our first chapter, we brought out the role of prayer (not only petitions, but a life alive with God) to help us accept our suffering and to be transformed by it. One hears acceptance and transformation in the prayer of Job:

> *The Lord gave and the Lord has taken away;*
> *Blessed be the name of the Lord!* (Job 1:21)

Upsetting Phrases

Before reflecting on the relationship of the mystery of creation to the mystery of suffering, I need to express my strong feelings concerning two sayings people frequently express to a suffering person.

The Will of God

The phrases "It is the will of God" or, "God wills it, even if we do not understand God's will," are often used correctly in some situations, but too often they are misused and/or are an abuse of the term.

We cannot state that it is God's will when someone who is drinking liquor to excess decides to drive, with the tragic result that your child, spouse, parent, or all of them are no longer alive. It is not the will of God when some egomaniac starts a civil war that results in the death of over 100,000 men, women, and children. It is not the will of God when we pollute the environment with carcinogens and toxic wastes. It is not the will of God when we smoke, eat, and drink too much, and end up with serious health problems. In Heaven, there is no cancer, no suffering, no death, because in Heaven God's will is fully realized. Furthermore, Jesus, as the revelation of God's will for us, did not go about making the healthy, sick; the ambulatory, lame; those with sight, blind. Jesus was sent by God to save, to heal, to make whole.

Someone observed that 46.7 percent of all statistics are made up. Did you know that 93.5 percent of all the evil in the world comes from people's free will? It is completely untrue and unfair to use the expression "It is God's will" in most cases of suffering.

Is it not amazing that people speak as if the Lord appeared to them personally and commanded them to inform a terminally ill patient that it is definitely God's will they are afflicted? How hurtful it must be for an already weakened, seriously sick person to be inflicted with the declaration that God wants the person to have this illness. While many will patiently listen to such declarations and somehow respond graciously, people like me get hugely upset by it. Maybe I need to understand that it is merely an inept attempt to help the sufferer accept the situation.

God's Punishment

"God punishes us because of our sins." I do not believe that God punishes us for our sins; our sins punish us and cause terrible dire consequences that we and others must bear. What I have in mind as an example is the mid-air explosion of TWA flight 800 minutes after it took off from Kennedy Airport, Long

Island, in July 1996. Do we think the 236 persons on board were being punished for their sins? Did God will that disaster to punish the American people for our consumerism, our materialism? I believe that God's heart was the first to break when the plane exploded.

In the Hebrew Scriptures, people did not make distinctions between "causing" and "allowing." Since God is all-powerful, they believed that God had to be the cause of everything. If God caused something bad to happen, God had a reason, and that reason must be punishment for sins. The Book of Job was written to challenge these assumptions. Job concludes that our finite minds cannot comprehend the Infinite designs of God.

While today we understand the distinction between causing and allowing, people still search for a cause or situation that might have put God in the position of allowing the evil to happen. Faith seeks understanding. In an attempt to find some reason for a loved one's suffering and to give it value and meaning, some believe that God would allow a life to be taken to prevent some future calamity. For example, if a loved one dies of cancer, God has allowed it to bring about some future blessing.

Underneath such searching lies the belief that someone must be blamed when bad things happen. For those who will not blame God, somebody's or their own behavior must be the cause. This means that the sufferer had to pay the price of appeasing God in order to move God to deal kindly towards others.

In reality, however, our God is a compassionate God whose Son taught us not to link suffering as punishment for our sins. Jesus, by his words (see below) and by his death on the cross, taught the reverse of suffering as punishment for sins. The saints, moreover, are forewarned to expect to suffer greatly.

At that time, some were present who told him about the Galileans whose blood Pilate had mixed with their sacrifices. He said in reply: "Do you think that these Galileans were the greatest sinners in Galilee just because they suffered this? By no means! But I tell you, you will all come to the same end unless you reform. Or take those eighteen who were killed by a falling tower in Siloam. Do you think they were more guilty than anyone else who lived in Jerusalem? Certainly not! But I tell you, you will all come to the same end unless you reform. (Luke 13:1–5)

I have told you all this to keep your faith from being shaken. Not only will they expel you from synagogues; a time will come when anyone who puts you to death will claim to be serving God! All this they will do to you because they know neither the Father nor me. But I have told you these things that when their hour comes you may remember my telling you of them. (John 16:1–4)

The Creator's Presence in a New World View

Ellen, please continue to reflect with me as we touch upon the relationship of creation to the mystery of suffering. The fascinating description of Creation in the book of Genesis with its cosmology (God dwelling in the heavens beyond the stars, the creatures of darkness residing below the earth, the earth as the center of the universe, etc.) has given way to a cosmology equally fascinating and awesome. Scientists estimate there are 200 billion stars in our galaxy (the Milky Way), and that there are 200 billion galaxies in this universe, and there may be another entire universe. Not to be irreverent, but if Jesus ascended into Heaven beyond the stars at the speed of light, then he is still ascending because the universe extends for trillions and trillions of light years! Perhaps, we suspect (or believe) he is in another dimension outside our space and time.

Quantum physics forces us to view creation as not made up of solids and their properties, but as a dynamic field of mass and energy. Where is God in this field of energy? Is God the mind within the mind within the force that constantly energizes and governs our world? Quantum physics calls us to look anew at our understanding of creation, and we need to ask what God's relationship is to it.

Ellen, at this moment you are probably wondering when I will get to the point! These tidbits about galaxies and quantum physics are interesting, you may be thinking, but it's not clear what these theories contribute to an explanation of the mystery of suffering.

My point is the all-important point of our image of God and how God is present to Creation. Our image of a benign, elderly man with a long beard enthroned above the stars and looking down lovingly (*from a distance*, as the song goes) on this good creation, must give way to a God who is the reality that energizes an infinitely expanding universe. We need to adjust our image of God to reflect a God who is transcendent, and who is "Incomprehensible Mystery yet every-where obvious."

Perhaps, this would be a good time to tell you a story.

Once upon a time there was a little fish in a little pond upstream who kept hearing about the ocean, how marvelous the ocean was, how magnificently wide, incredibly deep, etc. So, the little fish one day set out in search of the ocean. It took the little fish many days and nights to travel down all the streams but, eventually, the fish entered a river and finally arrived at the ocean though the little fish didn't realize it. Going up to some really big fish, the little fish asked excitedly, "Could you help me reach the ocean?" One of the large ones answered, "This is the ocean, you are in it now." The little fish was puzzled and replied, "But this is only water."

Contemporary theology moves us toward an encounter with the infinite ocean of being that already surrounds us and envelops us. Our God is nearer to us than we are to ourselves. We sometimes do not "see" God because, as someone said, it is like looking at your own eyes. Our God is Incomprehensible Mystery everywhere obvious, to those who look for the intimations of God.

In her poem "Aurora Leigh," the Victorian poet Elizabeth Barrett Browning gives poetic expression to this:

> *Earth's crammed with heaven*
> *and every common bush afire with God;*
> *But only those who see take off their shoes,*
> *the rest sit round it and pluck blackberries.*
> (adapted)

In the words of the Jesuit poet Gerard Manley Hopkins in "God's Grandeur":

> *The world is charged with the grandeur of God.*
> *It will flame out, like shining from shook foil.*

Our understanding of God calls us to see God as Mystery Present but not present in the world as a pilot in the cockpit of a plane, a skipper at the helm, or a person in a car with hands on the wheel to direct the course of it and to prevent accidents and tragedies. As with a composition by Beethoven, Beethoven provided the score, but he is not in the score or in the music guaranteeing its perfect performance. God has created us with intelligence and free will so that we are truly free to interpret Beethoven as we see it and to play it as we decide to play it. Likewise, we are free to interpret life and decide how we are going to live it.

God Says Yes to Creation

The mystery of creation means that God respects creation's nature and laws, and, ordinarily, does not suspend them when a bad thing is about to happen to an innocent person. God does not say no to creation in order to say yes to a prayer of deliverance.

Ellen, I make such an issue of understanding these few thoughts on creation because it is a major piece in the puzzle of life and suffering. It fits alongside, and must be joined to, our thoughts on the use and abuse of the expression "it is God's will" as well as our thoughts of suffering as punishment for sins. God created (creates) a world that is good, but God entrusted that world to creatures who are made in God's image and likeness and who possess free will. They can choose to live according to God's will by keeping the Commandments and following the Golden Rule, or they can decide to go their own way to the detriment of themselves and many others.

The evil in the world does not come from God. Jesus came to save us from all the evil, not by removing it or explaining it away, but by embracing it and conquering it. When tragedy strikes, the Spirit of

God is present to help us accept and transform it into our salvation. Whether the tragedy stems from our free will or from a source outside our control (earthquakes, hurricanes, etc.), God's way of answering our prayer is the always available, victorious presence of grace.

Miracles — God Saying Yes to Prayer

Having stated that God ordinarily says yes to creation and to its laws and nature, there is an obvious need to discuss miraculous healings. First, creation itself operates according to a rather high rate of predictability. But we also know that there are many instances of unforeseen and uncontrollable happenings in nature itself. Nature surprises us sometimes with the unexpected. Things happen by chance, even though nature is far from being a crap-shoot. Therefore, while most cancerous tumors tend to grow at their normal pace, some cancerous tumors have stopped growing and eventually disappear all on their own (or, at least, not because of treatment). So, not all tumors that disappear demand a miracle. Creation does not always need to work as precisely as a Swiss watch. We must, instead, have an image of creation running as dependably and predictably as the Japanese rail system.

Secondly, we believe that Jesus was a wonder-worker who made the blind see, the lame walk, etc. After the Spirit came down upon the apostles at Pentecost, they went forth and cured many people. There is the remarkable incident in Acts of the Apostles where even the shadow of Simon Peter heals someone! When we read these accounts in the Scriptures, we wonder whether these same extraordinary signs of God's power continue to exist in our times. The answer is yes; extraordinary signs have taken place. Let us take a look at some examples of such healing instances.

Besides the authenticated cases of cures at Lourdes and the confirmed miracles reported in canonizations of saints, most of us are personally aware of reported cases of cures associated with the healing ministry of such people as Kathryn Cullman, Fr. Ralph DiOrio, Sister Briege McKenna, and others.

A Franciscan Sister in Buffalo told our retreat group the story of her brother's cure. When her brother was five years old, he contracted a polio virus that almost took his life and left him with atrophied muscles in his left leg that prevented him from running well or playing competitive sports. When he was thirty-eight years old and married with two children, he and his wife traveled to Toronto to a

Kathryn Cullman healing service. Nothing extraordinary happened to him during the service. He
remarked to his wife on their way home to Buffalo
that the service was a beautiful, prayerful occasion
and that he was glad he had gone even though his
prayer for a physical healing had not been answered.

Two weeks later, his Franciscan sister, a nurse at a
hospital in Ohio, came for a visit. After dinner, she
watched in amazement as her brother walked
perfectly normally across the living room! He told his
sister that every day for seven days following the
healing service, he felt his condition improve and
entirely disappear. She couldn't believe that muscles
atrophied for over thirty years would again function
normally. She believes that God healed her brother
through the ministry of Kathryn Cullman.

My own encounter with a similar situation
occurred during a retreat I was preaching to a group
of Sisters. Midway through the week, we celebrated
the Mass of the Anointing of the Sick. After the
homily, we blessed the oils and I anointed the Sisters.
I experienced nothing special during the anointing.
One week later, I received a letter from one of the
Sisters who participated in the anointing. She wrote
that she had been depressed and had not wanted to
come to the retreat. In May, she had been honored as

teacher of the year in her diocese. By July, she had developed a throat ailment that reduced her speaking (and teaching) capacity to a whisper. Was this some mean joke by God, she had thought? She was angry at life, at her doctors, herself, and God.

How could she spend a week in prayer at her community's retreat? She came because she felt it easier to attend than to explain why she did not want to participate. Coming now to the Anointing Mass, she debated whether or not she was an apt candidate for the Sacrament. When push came to shove, she walked forward to be anointed. As she stood up to move to the center aisle, she suddenly experienced a warmth throughout her body. It startled her, yet she knew that she had to keep walking down the aisle for the Anointing. Now came the strange yet beautiful part. In her letter, the Sister described my face as radiant and my eyes the shiniest and bluest she had ever seen. A little bit of heaven came through the blue in those eyes, she said, for she was touched by God at that moment and her throat condition disappeared. Praise the Lord! A month later we arranged a meeting, and she was again struck speechless when she looked into my sometimes brown and sometimes green but never blue, hazel eyes!

Besides God continuing to work wonders of physical healings in striking ways through miracles or extraordinary happenings, God's healing presence lives and moves in very ordinary ways. Not only does it move through doctors and medicines but also through the tender loving touch of a caring person. Studies confirm the importance of touch for the health and growth of premature infants. While loving touches cannot cure cancer, they can sometimes work more effectively than some medicines.

How the touch of a caring person can affect the life and health of another we do not exactly know. In the Gospel of Luke we read that Jesus turned and asked who had touched him for power had gone out of him. Is there a power of healing in us? Is it possible that our prayers themselves, our loving desire to heal a loved one or any person, can be instruments of healing?

There are more questions concerning the presence of healing energy in creation than there are answers. Suffice it to say for now that God ordinarily says yes to creation and its nature and laws but that God has willed certain interventions to cure some people through miracles. Why some people are cured by a miracle and other people are not I cannot begin to understand and leave it to the incomprehensibility of God. We do know being cured does not mean one person is loved more than another, for God allowed Jesus to be crucified after he prayed for deliverance.

In years to come, we may have a clearer understanding of the power for healing that seems to be part and parcel of the energy that constitutes creation.

We Are God's Yes

Ellen, let me conclude by simply confessing that I do grow tired of thinking about the mystery of suffering from a philosophical or theological viewpoint. We will never find an answer to the question of how a loving God can allow, not cause, bad things to happen to good people. In the end, what remains for us is to be present to those who suffer and to grow in our ability and skills to bring comfort, maintain hope, and sustain faith. While stories of miraculous cures make for big headlines, the family, relatives, and friends who accompany their loved ones in their suffering, give witness to the Incomprehensible Mystery (God) yet everywhere obvious, everywhere present.

When my brother Neil's cancer dictated a leg amputation, his world, and that of the Lanahans, was shaken to its foundation. The last six months of Neil's life were a nightmare of pain. Even twenty-seven years later I cannot dwell on the memories without breaking down in tears.

Even though Rabbi Harold Kushner, author of *When Bad Things Happen to Good People*, advises us not to ask the question why bad things happen, we still ask why they had to happen to Neil. He was such a good person, and was taking care of our mother. We asked ourselves why it was not one of us religious, who, at least back twenty-five years ago, had another to take our place in the school or on the nursing staff. It was our nearest and dearest neighbor, Gen McCutcheon, who reminded me of why Neil, at only forty-four years of age and such a good, decent person was dying. Only God, said Gen McCutcheon, knew why Neil had been saved during his tour of duty in Korea. Only God knew why Neil had survived the car crash on New Year's morning when he fell asleep at the wheel. Probably, Gen said, there were many other close calls for Neil during his life. Gen's answer was a gem and a grace for me.

Without detailing all the events in Neil's last six months, it is enough to say that people came forward "miraculously" with extraordinary generosity and compassion to be with Neil and our sorrowful mother. I came July and August to be with him before and after the operation to help him bathe, change his bandages, dress, and go back and forth to the Kessler Institute where he was being fitted for a prosthesis and receiving physical therapy. Peggy came every weekend and holidays to cook and clean, to keep my mother and Neil company and their spirits bright even though Peggy's heart was heavy and breaking. Maureen came whenever she could, and fortunately was there to make the decision for Neil to go to the hospital for the last few days of his life.

Ellen, Abraham Maslow speaks of "peak experiences," where people feel connected with life or one with the whole universe, and, maybe, with the God of the universe and of life. Neil's suffering and death was about as far from a "peak" experience as one could be, yet it was a connecting with God, a solidarity with all suffering humanity. The Incomprehensible Mystery is everywhere obvious, or at least discernible by those of us who lived through it. God's presence in the "angels" who came to minister to Neil (and us) made an indelible impression on me and made me a believer in a living God who does not take away or explain away our suffering, but allows people to suffer—although never alone and never without God's conquering, saving presence.

❧

❧ 3: The Will of God, Your Salvation

Jesus did not come to explain away suffering or remove it. He came to fill it with his presence.
—Paul Claudel

Dear Dan,

Peace! Thanks for all you wrote about the mystery of suffering. It was hard in parts to digest, especially when you started to speak about God as "the Incomprehensible Mystery yet everywhere obvious"! Give me a break! I'll take "Our Father who art in heaven" any day! Can you imagine praying: "O, Incomprehensible Mystery, help me pass my driver's test today"? Yet, I realize we need

*to adopt new images and new language in the light
of contemporary theology and cosmology. Dan, I
have one last question and it is a humdinger. No one
has ever been able to explain it in any satisfying
way: Why did Jesus have to die on the cross? It is
one thing to wonder how a benevolent God could
allow, not cause, bad things to happen to good
people, but how could a loving God and Father not
only allow but will such a death for His Beloved
Son? Now, that is what I call "incomprehensible"!*

Your Pain pen pal,
Ellen

EVERYONE SHOULD HAVE a pal like you, Ellen, to
journey with, to share their pain in bad times, and to
challenge them to make some sense of the mysteries
of life. Sorry about trying to sneak in without warning
Karl Rahner's description of God as "Incomprehensible Mystery yet everywhere obvious."

Many theologians of the past had a passion for
providing us with a clear understanding of the truths
of faith through precisely defined terms and distinctions, objectively proposed, without directly
addressing the emotional level. Rahner and his ilk,
certainly, try to explain precisely the deep truths of
faith; however, they try to lead us to the top of a

mountain where they leave us in the clouds of the Unknowable, the Unfathomable, the Incomprehensible Mystery. If you fail to understand or accept my impression of Karl Rahner and company, press your cancel button and read on!

Let me summarize what I have written so far about the mysteries of suffering and creation and the purpose of prayer. These are the crucial points to keep in mind as we delve into the significance of our Lord's death on the cross.

1) Suffering is part of life whether its cause is human or natural.

2) God does not ordinarily intervene in creation to prevent suffering.

3) The purpose of prayer is not to change God, but to change us to accept, transform, and be transformed by the suffering.

4) God does not ordinarily deliver us from suffering but is present with power to enable us to bear the unbearable.

5) At the end of all philosophical and theological debate over the mystery of suffering, there is only one thing that remains — to be present to the sufferer with skills to assist and comfort, and with love and faith to journey with them to victory.

These five statements have been affirmed with some modifications by Catholics and non-Catholics for ages. Buddha's first truth of his Four Noble Truths is that life is suffering, and the second one is that we cause it by our greedy, selfish, willful desires. While Christians pray to move to acceptance of what we cannot change, Buddha's third truth urges us to pursue his way of enlightenment, which are eight ways to put to death our desires. Where Christians tend to part company with Buddha is on our point five. While Buddhists achieve great patience with suffering and are compassionate, they do not place the same emphasis on ministry or being caregivers.

Rabbi Harold Kushner believes in the power of prayer and the call to be present to those who suffer, as he and his wife cared for their son, Aaron, who died as a teenager from a rare malady. Kushner believes that God does not intervene to prevent suffering; in fact, he holds, along with process theologians, that God is not able to intervene. Herein lies the major reason why his book *When Bad Things Happen to Good People* was unable to satisfy my search for an answer to the question: Where is God when bad things happen to good people? While I believe that God does not ordinarily intervene to prevent suffering, the God I believe in is not only capable of intervening, but also capable of willingly entering into this world. God has become one of us in the person of Jesus. For Christians, Jesus is God's answer, God's word on suffering. In Christ, God said yes to our prayers. Now, to explain God's answer.

The Incarnation

Before we focus on the last events of Christ's life, the Cross, we need to ask what role the previous thirty years of his life played with regard to the mystery of human suffering.

The question that has haunted the human race from the beginning can be expressed simply: Does God care what happens to us on planet Earth? Did God create our planet and send it off spinning through the galaxies with a blessing: "Good luck, watch out for the other planets, try to avoid collisions"? The Incarnation is God saying, "Yes, I do care." The greatest proof of God's love for us is the Incarnation. Jesus became one of us and accepted everything we will ever experience or suffer (at least, in essence) and out of love for us drank the chalice of our existence to its dregs on the cross.

Several years ago, a number of Friars of Holy Name Province were invited to submit a short list of the names of the books, besides the Bible, that had

had the most profound influence on their lives. My first choice was Johannes Baptist Metz's slim volume, *Poverty of Spirit*. Why? Because it taught me a new understanding of the Incarnation, in particular, what the Beatitude "poor in spirit" means, and how it relates to our everyday lives.

Let me relate the circumstances of my life when I began to read *Poverty of Spirit*. In 1974, we relocated Christ the King Seminary from the campus of St. Bonaventure University in Allegany, New York, to East Aurora in the same state. In doing so, we changed from being in one very large three-story building to being on a seventeen-building campus. These buildings were spread out over 135 acres, and, for the most part, each building had one main purpose. There were six dormitories, a classroom building, a library, a chapel, a gym, etc.

These buildings were placed in this fashion as a statement of sharp contrast with the old seminaries and their castle-like appearance. One envisions seminarians of old crossing the moat, entering into these rock-like fortresses, never to be seen again until their ordination! The new seminary would necessitate getting outdoors as you made your way to chapel, classes, and the gym. It was definitely an excellent concept, providing many healthy physical and mental advantages.

There was one big flaw in the planning. East Aurora lies directly in the path of the snow-belt that cuts across upstate New York. Six months of the year, it was a pleasure to walk about the campus. The other six months, it was "curse the planners" time! They had sinned against the light! They should have built this type of seminary in Florida! We would come up with some options: Plan A—we spend the Fall semester in East Aurora, the Spring semester at St. Vincent's Seminary in Boynton Beach. Plan B—build tunnels between the buildings.

Reality and God's Will

It was during the blizzard of 1977 when Metz's *Poverty of Spirit* spoke to me: "Daniel, some day you may be in warm, sunny Florida, but right now you are in the snow and ice of a Buffalo winter. The most Christ-like response you can make is to accept your present existence, snow boots and all!" This conversion did not change the wintry conditions, but it changed my attitude. I learned from *Poverty of Spirit* that to be poor in spirit is to accept and embrace the human condition with the circumstances in which you find yourself.

In emptying himself and becoming one of us, Jesus willingly accepted the human condition. The Evangelists' accounts of the three temptations in the desert make it clear that Jesus would not "break out" of the limits of the condition of being human to use his divine power to turn rocks into bread or to save himself from the laws of gravity. He stayed within the limits of being human. In his ministry, he did perform miracles but not for his own benefit.

As Metz powerfully captures it, the Cross is the sacrament of poverty of spirit. Jesus was asked to be unfaithful to being human: "Come down from the cross if you really are the Son of God." (Matt. 27:40) Jesus remained faithful to his poverty of spirit, to the reality of his Incarnation into the human condition.

When I realized for the first time the true meaning and challenge of being poor in spirit, I knew then that it means to imitate Christ by wholeheartedly accepting whatever comes my way. It does not mean just grinning and bearing one's situation, so that God will reward you with Heaven one day. It means to choose the situation as God's will for you. We ask often what God's will is for us. Most of the time we do not need to spend long hours on a mountaintop to discern God's will. It usually is, as the popular expression puts it, "in your face." God's will is to accept and embrace the challenges, the joys and sorrows, the aches and pains of our everyday existence. Herein is the proper use of the phrase — it is God's will. It is not that God wills the suffering (most of it comes from human origins); God's will is for us to face reality and embrace it without allowing it to conquer us. Whenever bad things happen to us, we should do everything we can to deliver ourselves from them, including praying for a miracle and removing ourselves from abusive situations. However, once we have done all that we are able to do, the will of God is for us to accept the reality of the suffering.

It is not always easy to accept our existence. When we receive a promotion or a pleasant surprise, we readily echo Mary's "let it be done unto me according to your will." When cancer, the death of a loved one, or the loss of our livelihood happens, we find it harder to accept. We do not easily or quickly move to utter Job's words: the Lord giveth and the Lord taketh. Blessed be the Lord! (Job 1:20)

Interestingly, when my friend Gail learned that I was in the process of writing this book, she sent a note of encouragement. It was a delightful surprise because it pointed to the challenge of being "poor in spirit."

*I want to wish you well in the writing of your book.
It certainly is an engaging premise "When God
Says No," and it will be insightful to read your
thoughts and experiences. As one who doesn't take
No very well, even when it comes from God, I am
looking forward to reading it. Hopefully, it will help
me choose better responses and learn a more
gracious acceptance of "what is"!*

The Hidden Years of Jesus of Nazareth

For the longest time, I wondered why Jesus spent so
many years in Nazareth and just a few short years
preaching his mission. Concerning his so-called
"hidden years," I used to imagine Jesus as an actor
who was waiting in the wings. When his public
ministry began, he came on stage and began to
interact with the other players. His triumphal entry
into Jerusalem meant that he came front and center
stage. His death and resurrection were the climax of
the drama of salvation.

It is absolutely true that our salvation reached its
climax with his death and resurrection. What is
equally true and essential to our faith, is that everything that Jesus did, from the moment of his
conception in the womb of Mary to his being nailed to
the cross, all the good he did and all the evil he

endured, climaxing with his crucifixion and resurrection, brought about our salvation.

This has profound significance. It means that everything in our daily life over the years, all the joy and sorrow, are not lost, useless, or unimportant. When we, in imitation of Jesus, accept what comes our way and embrace it as the will of God, that situation becomes for us an intimate participation in our salvation. When we are "poor in spirit," we reincarnate Jesus again in the world and make up what was lacking in the sacrifice of Christ. His sacrifice was perfect; what was lacking was our participation in the suffering.

In making this point about accepting what comes our way as the will of God, it must be clearly understood that Jesus never taught that we are to stay in situations that are abusive or violent. If our situation is abusive or violent, it is the will of God to do whatever we have to do to right the wrong of the situation. Jesus does not recommend anyone being a doormat and having his or her human dignity stepped on.

Practically speaking, the lesson we learn from Jesus' so-called "hidden years" is this: Unless we live a life of poverty of spirit, we will not be able to cope with cancer or another deadly disease when it afflicts us. We need to live a life of acceptance of our daily crosses if we want to be able to cope with the heavier crosses of suffering. St. Paul wrote that Jesus learned obedience through suffering. It means that his faithfulness to accepting everyday life led him to bear the unbearable during his Passion. We must realize how our whole life is a preparation for our death.

The Eucharist, the Sacrament of the Everyday

Does God care what goes on in our everyday life? The Incarnation is God answering yes. The yes of the Incarnation continues down through the centuries in the great gift of the Eucharist. On the night before Jesus was lifted high on the cross, he knew the "hour" had come for him to pass from this life to Glory. He wanted to return to Heaven, yet he desired to remain with us, so he gave us the Eucharist. Now he is at the right hand of God and is still with us. God so loved the world that God continues to give Jesus in Word and sacramental flesh and blood for our salvation.

God continues to save us from the belief that the Creator does not really care what happens to us in our everyday lives of joys and sorrows. Whenever, in the Eucharist, we eat this Bread and drink this Cup, we proclaim the loving service that Jesus did on Calvary. His sacrifice is made present again, so that we can unite our sufferings to his. Not only are the bread and wine changed into the Body and Blood of Jesus, but our everyday acceptance of our joys and sorrows are also transformed and caught up in the Eucharist in an infinite act of worship and redeeming service on behalf of the whole human race.

Through the mystery of the Incarnation and the Eucharist we see more clearly what Paul Claudel meant when he wrote: "Jesus did not come to explain away suffering or remove it. He came to fill it with his presence." Through his Incarnation, Jesus embraced our everyday existence and made it holy by filling it with his presence. Through the Eucharist, he continues to make our everyday life sacred by transforming it with his presence.

Keeping in mind the importance of the entire life of Jesus, we are better prepared to understand why Jesus willingly accepted death on the cross.

The Passion and Death of Jesus

More than any other Evangelist, John leads us directly into the heart of the matter of Jesus and suffering.

Jesus said to Nicodemus, "Just as Moses lifted up the serpent in the desert, so must the Son of Man be lifted up, that all who believe may have eternal life

in him. Yes, God so loved the world that he gave his
only Son, that whoever believes in him may not die
but have eternal life. God did not send his Son into
the world to condemn the world, but that the world
might be saved through him." (John 3:14–17)

Nicodemus had come to Jesus at night to try to grasp what Jesus was all about. He openly called Jesus a man of God yet wondered why Jesus was so strongly opposed to the religious leaders and why, in particular, Jesus would disrupt the Temple services by knocking over the merchants' tables and chasing them out of that area of the Temple. Perhaps Nicodemus was advising Jesus to ease up on his opposition or he would pay the consequences of being put on trial, found guilty, and being sentenced to death. It was at that point that Jesus spoke.

Certainly, Nicodemus had no understanding of why "the Son of Man," Jesus, *must* be lifted up on the cross, so that we may have eternal life. I confess that I too did not understand the reason until very recently. Again, it is John's Gospel that brings out the reason clearly.

Do you remember the strange scene in the Garden when the mob comes out to arrest Jesus? It is night, the time when the powers of darkness make their move (John 18). Notice how in John Jesus is in full command:

> *Jesus, aware of all that would happen to him [the Cross], stepped forward and said to them, "Who is it you want?" "Jesus, the Nazorean," they replied. "I am he," he answered. As Jesus said to them, "I am he" they retreated slightly and fell to the ground. Jesus put the question to them again, "Who is it you want?" "Jesus the Nazorean," they repeated. "I have told you, I am he," Jesus said.* (John 18:4–8)

This time, the soldiers do not retreat or fall to the ground but advance and arrest Jesus. John told this incident so that it was clear to the mob and to all of us who are his disciples that the forces of darkness, the powers of evil, did not put Jesus to death. He willingly surrendered himself to them.

We know what followed: They falsely accused him, whipped him, spat on him, placed a crown of thorns on him, sentenced him to death, and made him carry his own cross on the way to his crucifixion, where they ended the excruciating ordeal by piercing his side with a lance. Why did Jesus allow them to do this to him; why did he willingly suffer so cruelly at the hands of the powers of darkness, the forces of evil? Jesus did so because he wanted to be in solidarity and communion with every man, woman, and child down through the centuries who has ever been falsely accused, tortured, spat upon, ridiculed, stripped naked, violated, or unjustly put to death in the most hideous forms of execution.

After Jesus had died, Nicodemus was one who helped bury him. Can't you hear Nicodemus saying, "I tried to warn him that they were out to do him in"? Poor Nicodemus had no idea, nor could anyone have expected it, but in three days Jesus was once more walking among them. The powers of darkness, forces of evil, and sin had done their worst to him. When someone is being attacked, they usually put their hands in front of their face to protect themselves. When Jesus bore the assault of others, he stretched out his arms and allowed them to take their best shot. They thought they had conquered him, but God raised him up victoriously.

Jesus, the Son of Man, had to be lifted up on the cross so that he would be in solidarity with all who have suffered. However, we need to keep in mind, especially as we look upon his crucified body and see his blood, that we must look beyond the Cross to the Resurrection. "And if Christ has not been raised, our preaching is void of content and your faith is empty too." (1 Cor. 15:14)

What precisely does Jesus save us from?

Rescue from Fear

Jesus rescues us from the dreadful fear that this life is all there is — that when it's over, it's over. We have often heard that sickness and death are the result of sin. This is not true. Sickness and death are essential parts of life. Everything living has its beginning, its development to maturity, and its eventual disintegration and death. Error enters into life when it instills in us an inordinate fear of sickness and death. How does such a fear enter into our lives? If someone thinks that this life is all there is — and, let's face it, it's a very popular belief in our society — then, you can readily understand why sickness and suffering threaten that existence and why, of course, death would be disastrous: it would end everything. Hence, the fear of sickness and death becomes inordinate.

The Fathers and Mothers of the Church offered a beautiful image to help allay people's fear. They taught that we should not be inordinately fearful of death because we have already had an experience with it. Most of us lived for nine months in our mother's womb where all our needs were taken care of and where we enjoyed a swimmingly good time. However, the ninth month arrived, when it was detrimental to our mother and for us to stay in her womb. So, we died to that world, entered into the birth canal, and came out into this bigger womb, this larger world, where all our needs are not always taken care of. The Church teaches that no matter how long we live in this new world, whether it is one year, five years, or 105 years, each of us is going to face another ninth month when we will die to this world and enter into a new, more beautiful world. In this world, however, there will be no more suffering, no more dying, and we will live with our Creator and all our loved ones forever.

A Resurrection Parable

A modern parable addresses the same fear in a beautiful fashion.

> *Once upon a time, twins were conceived in the same womb. As time passed, they grew and began to have feelings and some idea of their surroundings.*
>
> *One said, "Lucky are we to have been conceived and to have this world." The other said, "Blessed is the Mother who gave us this life and each other."*

Arms grew and fingers, legs, and toes. The twins explored their world and found the cord which gave them life from the precious Mother's blood. So they sang: "How great is the Mother that she shares all that she has with us." And they were pleased and satisfied with their lot.

Months passed and they noticed changes.

"We are changing. What can it mean?"

"It means that birth is coming near."

Fear crept over them. Birth meant that they had to leave all their world behind them.

"If it were up to me, I'd live here forever," said one.

"We must be born," said the other. "See the scars? There were others here before us. Maybe there's life after birth."

"How can there be life after birth? Have you ever talked to anyone who's been born? Has anyone ever re-entered the womb after birth? This life is absurd if it all ends in birth. If this is so, then there really is no Mother."

"But of course there is a Mother. Who else gives us nourishment and this world?"

"We get our own nourishment and our world has always been here. If there is a Mother, where is

she? Have you ever seen her or talked to her? We just invented her because it makes us feel good!"

And so one complained and despaired, but the other placed its trust in the hands of the Mother. Pretty soon the twins knew that birth was at hand. They were scared. They cried as they were born into the light. Then they opened their eyes and found themselves cradled in the warm love of the Mother. All too wonderful to believe.

(Author Unknown)

Jesus taught that those who believe in him, even if they die, will live forever. Jesus not only taught this, but lived it. He lived for nine months in the womb of Mary, his mother, and was born and lived some thirty-three years before he suffered, died, and rose from the dead. Jesus says to us all: Be not afraid, I go before you. By his resurrection, Jesus saved us from the dreadful fear that when this life is over, it's over. He revealed that this life is a prelude to Eternal Life, our real destiny, our final home. As St. Paul asked: "Death where is your sting? O Death, where is your victory?"

Rescue from Despair

Jesus saves us from the despair that life is inevitably tragic and suffering meaninglessness by revealing that our sufferings are united to his sufferings for our salvation and the salvation of others.

Through the ritual of Baptism we are in Christ and Christ is in us, so our sufferings are in him and his sufferings are united with ours. Knowing that our lives are connected to his life rescues us from the despair and our sense of meaninglessness. We hardly ever realize that our sufferings are united with his. Nor did he experience his sufferings of the Cross as being connected to anyone when he cried out, "Father, why have you abandoned me?" Maybe we more readily identify with Jesus in his abandonment rather than in his and our physical sufferings.

Rescue from Feelings of Insignificance

Jesus also saves us from the feeling or sense that we are insignificant, unimportant, and worthless. He does this by revealing that every person is of priceless worth. Jesus willingly laid down his life out of love for you and me. We are precious in his sight. While Jesus suffered excruciating physical and mental pain, it was his love, rather than the actual suffering, that redeemed and saved us. God did not will Jesus to suffer; people willed it ("God so loved the world"). Jesus so loved us that he would go to any extent, even crucifixion, to bring us peace, and lead us to the fullness of Life with our loving Creator.

Rescue from Feelings of Not Being Cared For

Lastly, Jesus saves us from the conviction that God does not care about us, that God created the world like a spinning top that was tossed out into the universe and wished well, but that we and our sufferings were promptly forgotten about. God cared so much that Jesus became one of us and suffered everything we will ever have to endure—at least, in essence—and he drank the chalice of our existence to its dregs on the cross out of love for us.

In summary, God in Jesus the Crucified said no to the dreadful fear that when life is over, it is over. He said no to the despair that life is inevitably tragic and suffering is meaningless. He said no to the sense that we are insignificant, unimportant, worthless. He said no to the conviction that God does not really care.

Instead, he said yes by helping us to see this life as a prelude to Eternal Life, our real home and destiny. He said yes by revealing that our sufferings are united to the sufferings of Christ for the salvation of the world. He said yes by revealing that every person is of priceless worth. He said yes by revealing our God as

Emmanuel (God with us). God cared enough to become one with us in the Incarnation.

> *God so loved the world that God gave God's only Son, that whoever believes in him may not die but may have eternal life. God did not send the Son into the world to condemn the world, but that the world might be saved through him.* (John 3:16–17)

∾

4: Jesus, the Saving Presence of Unconditional Love

Dear Dan,

Peace! What you wrote about Jesus saving us not only from the guilt of sin, but also from fear, despair, and abandonment by God deepened and widened my understanding of salvation. Most of the time I dwell on Jesus redeeming us by paying back by his death the debt incurred by the sin of Adam and Eve; he was our ransom for sin. To be honest, I am really uncomfortable when I think that God was so angry with us humans that the only way to appease God's wrath was the Cross. Please reflect further on the notion of salvation and redemption. I need you to do that.

> *Your grateful friend,*
> *Ellen*

ONE OF THE least satisfying parts of Christian theology, Ellen, concerns our teaching on redemption and salvation. We often use the terms interchangeably, even though salvation is a much broader term. The word redemption itself means to buy back or to ransom. As you expressed it, Jesus bought back God's friendship by washing away the guilt of sin by his blood on the Cross. Salvation is the grace-filled situation created by Jesus' redemptive death.

While it is true that this understanding of redemption as a kind of world-debt reduction is a central teaching of our faith and can be found easily and clearly in the Bible, it need not be the only valid, exclusive presentation of the mystery. In fact, it does seem to imply an awful image of God. I keep thinking that such an understanding of salvation comes from a more primitive culture and resembles more the behavior of patriarchs than the totally other, transcendent God who is, first of all, the author of salvation. How do we reconcile this angry image of God with John's "God so loved the world..."?

Salvation as Freedom

At the dawn of Christianity, there is the beautiful prophetic hymn of praise by Zechariah at the birth of John the Baptist. While Zechariah may primarily present the prophecy in terms of Israel's hope for liberation from political oppression, he does proclaim a rich notion of salvation as freedom from fear and guilt.

Blessed be the Lord, the God of Israel, who has come to set the People free. God has raised up for us a mighty savior, born of the house of David the servant. Through the prophets, God promised of old salvation from our enemies and all who hate us. God promised to show mercy to our forebears and to remember the Covenant.

This was the oath God swore: To set us free from the hands of our enemies, free to worship without fear, holy and righteous in God's sight all the days of our life.

You, my child, shall be called the prophet of the Most High; for you will go before the Savior to prepare the way, to give people knowledge of salvation by the forgiveness of their sins.

In the tender compassion of our God the dawn from on high shall break upon us, to shine on those

*who dwell in darkness and the shadow of death, and
to guide our feet into the way of peace."* (Luke
1:68–79, adapted)

Jesus came, first and foremost, that we may have
life and have it abundantly. To that end, he set us free
from the displeasure of God by being God's mercy.
More than anything else, Jesus set us free from fear—
free from the fear that, because we sinned against
God's holiness and justice, God no longer invites us to
the intimacy experienced by Adam and Eve when
they "walked with God in the cool of the evening," as
portrayed in Genesis.

The greatest fear of children of all ages is to be
abandoned by the ones who provide the security that
being loved brings. By becoming one of us, Jesus
wiped away the tears that flowed from our fear of
abandonment. By walking with us in the cool of a
Galilean evening as well as in the heat of the day, he
restored the intimacy we desired with all our hearts.
By shedding his blood on the cross, he washed away
our guilt. By rising from the dead, he restored our
hope and "guided our feet into the way of peace."
Jesus is our salvation.

By his life, death, and resurrection, Jesus revealed
that our God, in the words of St. Paul's hymn to

charity (1 Cor. 13) "is patient and kind, slow to anger...does not brood over injuries...is rich in compassion." As Paul wrote to Timothy, "the goodness and kindness of God has appeared" in the person of Jesus. For Paul, Jesus is the image of the Invisible God, the icon, the sacrament of God who never stopped loving us, never changed towards us even when we sinned and abandoned God. Jesus is the saving power of Unconditional Love.

Becoming the Saving Presence of Jesus

Salvation in Jesus is a priceless gift. But this gift carries an invitation with it. It contains a love demand. Jesus is the image of God, the *first* born of all creatures; in him is the fullness of grace. By his death and resurrection, Jesus has restored us to the fullness of being images of God, like himself. He invites us to become fully what we are created to be, the living images of God. Some people might prefer the word "icon" or "sacrament" to the concept of image. Whatever word we choose, the importance of being the "goodness and kindness" of God is what counts. When bad things happen to good people (as well as not-so-good people) God wants to be there, in and through us. How do we become the saving Presence of God to one another? Let us start by highlighting the beginning stages in Jesus' developing awareness of who he was and his mission of salvation.

The Baptism of Jesus

The importance of the baptism of Jesus cannot be overemphasized. In dramatic fashion, Mark captures the significance of the event (Mark 1:9–11). The heavens open and a dove, a symbol of God and a harbinger of peace, descends upon Jesus as he hears, "You are my beloved, in whom I am absolutely delighted." Overwhelmed by the experience, Jesus needs the solitude of the desert to grasp more clearly the significance of this manifestation, this particular epiphany of God's openness to the world. Jesus needs also to spend time contemplating and relishing the title, the Beloved. Forty days later, Jesus charges out of the desert, fired up with the mission to tell how openly in love God is with us and how God wishes us to realize that we are the beloved, the image of Jesus himself.

Our own baptism was probably less dramatic than our Savior's. No heavens opened, no dove descended, there was no voice from above. Yet, at that moment, we became the beloved in whom God is absolutely delighted. Our family and the community of beloveds, known also as the Church, had the privileged responsibility to help us grow in our awareness of who we are and the mission entrusted to us.

I Am the Beloved of God

Once upon a time, Wolfgang Amadeus Mozart was paid a visit by an admirer who asked him an unusual question, namely, if he was happy. You can imagine the situation. Mozart composed much joyous music and was admired by this contemporary of his. In the mind of the admirer rose the understandable question whether that successful and celebrated man had, in fact, found happiness. The admirer, I guess, was not quite happy; but a composer like Mozart is "supposed" to be happy.

After hesitating for a long time, the admirer asked the great question, expecting, even being almost sure, that the answer would be affirmative. The admirer may have perhaps been hoping that in Mozart's answer would lie a few hints that could show him the road to happiness. Then came Mozart's remarkable answer: "I am neither happy nor unhappy."

If we were to be asked the great question, what would we reply? Some of us might answer enthusiastically that we are extremely happy and totally contented with our life. Some might respond that we are deeply unhappy and completely discontented with everything in our life! Both groups of these people would tempt me to challenge them to make a one hundred percent honest evaluation of their lives.

When we take an honest look at our lives, I believe that most of us would say, "I do not know. In the beginning everything looked fine. I set some high goals and pursued them energetically. But, before too long, I began to lose my idealism and enthusiasm. I am not unhappy, but I can't say that an angel is always playing heavenly music in my heart. Things are normal and routine." While this response may sound very "realistic" and mature, it does not seem very fully engaged. When we think and talk this way, you can be sure that something is fundamentally wrong.

What might that be? To this question a lot of answers could be given. Basically, the philosophers of old would say that we are fired into this world with a certain madness, a certain restlessness, and that, therefore, we are never completely satisfied. There is always something good, beautiful, or pleasurable that we have not yet experienced. So, we are almost constantly in a state of dissatisfaction or unhappiness.

St. Augustine came along to teach us that there is no one thing, nor all things taken together, that can satisfy the human heart. Happiness is born out of something more profound, essential, and decisive.

What might that be? The most profound happiness, our ultimate happiness, is achieved when we exist in love, when we are conscious of being loved, and when we feel ourselves fulfilled in love. And the love meant here is not the love of just anyone. There are plenty of people who exist in love and who are still unfulfilled and essentially lonesome. No matter how great human love is, people know there is still something missing.

The ultimate explanation of our dissatisfaction must be that we have been planned, projected, and made for something deeper, something more essential. Yes, we are destined for personal relationships with people in life; but the aim is that through them we finally encounter God, before whose face alone we realize our being, our profoundest fulfillment and deepest happiness. As Augustine prayed: "You have made us for yourself, O God, and our hearts are restless until they rest in you."

Our deepest need is to be loved by God. The beginning of all human and Christian existence starts with the realization that we are loved by God. As Khalil Gibran wrote, we exist in and under God's love "as a parched land beneath a gentle rain, as a flower in the sun, as a beloved beneath the caresses of a spouse."

Henri Nouwen's *The Life of the Beloved* stresses the importance of knowing that we are loved by God. He strongly advises that, before we listen to those who love us dearly and before we listen to those who criticize us negatively, we must first listen in prayer to the soft voice of God whispering to us the words spoken to Jesus in the Jordan: You are my beloved, in whom I am absolutely delighted (a paraphrase of Nouwen's words).

Nouwen urges us to claim and to hold on dearly to the title, the beloved. With the recent biographies of Nouwen revealing his struggle with depression and loneliness, his stress on believing in God's love takes on added significance.

There is a simple devotional practice we might find valuable. For two minutes in the morning and two minutes at night, we should say to ourselves: "I am the beloved of God. I am the beloved of God." We should keep saying it for two minutes without any self-commentary (e.g. Who me?). We need to be faithful to this simple devotion until the realization moves from our head to our heart. Some believe that the trip from the head to the heart is the greatest distance in the world.

Sin and Suffering Challenge a Beloved

Ellen, not everyone worries whether God loves them or not, but there are many people who believe that God does not love them. Besides perfectionists who think they have to be perfect to be loved, there are two groups of people who predictably struggle with believing they are beloved by God.

The first are people who are haunted by some past shameful and sinful behavior. They may have expressed their sorrow to the people they hurt, and asked pardon; they may have confessed their sorrow to God and asked for forgiveness. Yet, they cannot let go of the memory of the behavior, and therefore allow it to define who they are.

We Americans pride ourselves on being great managers; we thrive on initiating effective ways to resolve problems. It is definitely a valuable asset in earning a living. When it comes to the spiritual life and our relationship with God, however, the first thing we need to do is to allow God to do something for us and to us. We need to let God show us mercy. We need to believe the words of Isaiah that, when God forgives us, God throws our sins over His shoulder, never to look at them again. We need to take to heart Isaiah's powerful message and image of God's purifying mercy: "Even if your sins are as red as scarlet, I will make them as white as snow."

There can be many reasons why we might hold onto our sins and keep defining ourselves by them. One of the most subtle reasons that is difficult to address is not forgiving ourselves. We often believe deep down that God has really forgiven us; but we, ironically, cannot or will not forgive ourselves. Again, there can be many reasons keeping us from forgiving ourselves. Perhaps, the most basic reason may be that we have not yet arrived at an unconditional acceptance of ourselves. We hopefully have been loved unconditionally by our parents or spouse or a friend. But, we need also to love ourselves unconditionally. While we tell ourselves that we are really a good person, capable of doing wonderful, kind deeds, we know also that we are capable of doing dumb, shameful, hurtful things. We convince ourselves that the real me is the wonderful loving me and not the one capable of hurting others. To love ourselves unconditionally, we need to accept the reality that the real me is a combination of the two. St. Paul speaks honestly about himself and all of us: There is in me the will to do good, but there is also in me the power to do what I do not want to do.

To forgive ourselves and allow the waters of God's purifying, regenerative mercy to wash away our sins is not an easy task. It is usually a slow process in which we gently close the door on a past that was more focused on ourselves and our sins and gently open the door to genuine peace and a more God-centered life.

The second category of people who often struggle to believe that God loves them are those good people who suffer tragedies in their lives or in the lives of those they love. They ask: "Why me? Why my loved one?" Often they believe in God, but believe that God does not care for them, has let them down, or has not been good to them (a goodness they deserve because of their commitment to Gospel living). It is definitely normal to react initially to bad news by questioning the reality of God's love for us.

In earlier chapters we addressed the issue of bad things being punishment for our sins and also the abuse of the phrase "it is God's will" that we suffer. Here we wish to tackle the question that remains when we have already accepted that God is not punishing us and it is not God's will that we are suffering. The very real question is: What does a person do when they are face to face with death, a terminal illness, serious birth defects, a baby with Down's syndrome, the death of a spouse, or loss of property or finances? What part does God play, if any, in these situations?

Get Busy Living or Get Busy Dying

The previous chapters contain our reflections on facing death. In particular, we dealt with the deaths of Jesus and of my brother, Neil. The following section centers on our coping with the sufferings that are part and parcel of life. We do not have to go in search of such troubles. Life leaves them on our doorstep.

When we learn that we have cancer or that our baby has Down's syndrome, or that our spouse and mother of our children has been killed in an accident, what do we do? Most people of faith begin to pray for help or a miracle from God. When the miracle doesn't happen, when God says no to our petition, we often stop praying, at least for a while. Then, many start praying again, but not using the familiar words or style of formal petitions. People of faith begin to talk to God about their suffering and their fears about the future. They come to realize that it is a time of crisis but also a time of growth in courage and hope.

Profiles in Courage

My father came from County Cork, Ireland to New York City at the end of the nineteenth century. There, he met and married Mary Fitzgerald. They proceeded to have seven children. A sword of sorrow pierced their hearts when their son, Tom, died as an infant. When the youngest child was about five years old, Mary's nightgown caught fire from one of those old cast-iron stoves. It happened late one Monday night; on Friday, forty-two year-old Mary died.

It took my dad four or five years to get his life together again. With the invaluable help of my half-brother's future wife, Mary Ward, the younger kids were well taken care of. My father could have become bitter because of the death of his much-loved wife, but he did not. After a fourteen-year period of adjustment and some financial prosperity, he married a pretty and very young Maggie Sheehan. With her, he raised a family of five. Since I am the youngest of the second batch, I am delighted that my father (we always called him Pop, because he was from Cork!) did not give up on life or God; instead, with hope, he had a very happy second marriage that celebrated its thirtieth anniversary.

While Pop Lanahan's life was special, it was also quite typical. Most people have had similar crosses to bear and some have had much heavier ones to carry. Recently, on one of the morning TV talk shows, a strikingly beautiful blonde with a radiant smile was invited to share her personal and courageous story of victory against great odds. She was born without legs and with only one arm. Would you believe that she is married and has a couple of children? What a remarkable profile in courage! More than anything else, the joy this woman possesses speaks volumes about facing reality with courage and hope.

When I was a teenager, I thought there were only three major challenges in life. To grow up into a mature and responsible adult was the one in which I was then presently engaged. Everybody was telling me to grow up! The second task was deciding what I was going to do with my life. Would I become an accountant, a tavern owner, a Yankee pitcher, or a Franciscan priest? Choosing to be a Franciscan eliminated the necessity of dealing with maverick Yankee owner George Steinbrenner as well as the third great challenge: to choose a wife and establish a family. In my youthful simplicity and naiveté, I believed that a person could and should tackle these challenges by the time they reached twenty-five or thirty years of age. I thought if I got these challenges out the way, the storm clouds and stress of these challenges would disappear permanently, and I would enjoy nothing but beautiful, tranquil blue skies from that time on! Now wasn't that unreal?

The first great truth of the Four Noble Truths of Buddha is that life is suffering. While there are many wonderful experiences in life, there are at least as many painful ones. The best image of life is the ocean. Some days it is calm, at other times it is relatively rough; and there are days, if you are in for a swim, where you will get knocked right off your feet. Isn't it true that life, like the ocean waves, just keeps coming at us?

What are we called to do? We are called to accept the fact that life is not bad, it is just the way life is. As in Robert Frost's poem "The Road Less Traveled," we all come to a divide in the road of life. We can choose to abandon hope and live life as a tragic victim, or we can take the road of hope and courage. It makes all the difference when we accept and embrace life as it comes with courage and hope and allow it to transform us.

In the movie *The Shawshank Redemption*, starring Tim Robbins and Morgan Freeman, there is the powerful statement uttered by one prisoner to a prisoner who has allowed depression and despair to dominate his life. His words should challenge all of us when bad things come our way: "You are either getting busy living or getting busy dying."

The will of God for us beloved sons and daughters is to get busy living. Whatever happens to us is part of our salvation, if we bear it with faith, hope, and love.

My Mission as the Beloved of God

To the end that salvation comes powerfully into our lives, two things are necessary. We must believe that we are the beloved of God, in whom God is absolutely delighted. Hopefully, the previous few pages have provided thoughts to nurture that realization in us. What is of equal importance, however, is that there is no salvation unless our love of God and God's love for us breaks out into loving service to others.

The Gospel story of Zacchaeus, a wealthy tax-collector hated by his people for exploiting them, illustrates clearly the dynamics of an individual's salvation. Zacchaeus desired to meet Jesus, but, because of the crowd and his shortness of stature, he could not. He then decided to climb a tree. When Jesus spotted the expensively dressed man in the tree, he, presumably with a smile, approached Zacchaeus with the request, "I would like to have dinner with you tonight." When the meal was over, the man was so moved by Jesus' regard for him that he promised to correct his fraudulent ways and even "to give half of my belongings to the poor." Jesus proclaimed, "today salvation has come to this house." (Luke 19)

The Richard Rogers/Oscar Hammerstein II musical *The Sound of Music* contains that wonderful line, "love isn't love until you give it away." Salvation isn't salvation until you give it away! Granted that when suffering first strikes us it necessarily makes us self-preoccupied. We and our family and professional assistants marshal our efforts and energy to concentrate on dealing with the situation. But, after a time, when a kind of routine sets in, we need to be drawn out of ourselves to look around us at others who are suffering (as well as to appreciate the caregivers).

Concern about others can run the gamut between a simple interest in the welfare of another to providing constant care. When my mother first went into a nursing home, she was unhappy, grieving the loss of her own home. Whenever I came for a visit, I would try to cheer her up with funny stories or jokes. Normally, I would not mention any bad or sad news about family and friends. Why burden her with more sadness?

Slowly I arrived at the idea that it might be good for my mother to learn about Aunt Nellie's latest heart attack or Uncle Tim's arthritis. When I asked her to pray for them or others, I noticed a significant change in her. When I would arrive for a visit, the first thing she would do would be to ask how Nellie and Tim were. The door of salvation and happiness opens out to care and concern for others.

Two days before my brother Neil died, he spoke to our sister Peggy, not about himself, but about his concern for our mother's financial security. Such a concern shows salvation in action. As Jesus spoke to his beloved John to take care of Mary, Neil transcended his painful agony in being concerned about another, our mother. Whenever we transcend our own suffering to reach out to another, we witness the saving power of love. Such reaching out to others is not only doing some good, but it is being caught up in the tremendous mystery of God's love for the world.

St. John summarizes our mission as a beloved in his first letter (1 John 4:7–12):

Beloved, let us love one another because love is of God; everyone who loves is begotten of God and has knowledge of God.The one without love has known nothing of God, for God is love. God's love was revealed in our midst in this way: God sent the Son to the world that we might have life through him.

*Love, then consists in this: Not that we have
loved God but that God has loved us and has sent
the Son as an offering for our sins.*

*Beloved, if God has loved us so, we must have
the same love for one another. No one has ever seen
God. Yet if we love one another God dwells in us,
and God's love is brought to perfection in us.*

An unknown author captures our mission of
salvation, not only concerning those suffering
physical or emotional illnesses, but also those
enduring economic deprivation.

*On the street I saw a small girl
Cold and shivering in a thin dress,
with little hope of a decent meal.
I became angry and said to God:
Why did you permit this?
Why don't you do something about it?
For a while God said nothing.
That night God replied quite suddenly:
"I certainly did something about it.
— I made you."*

5: How Neil's Suffering Touched Upon Our Lives

Dear Dan,

Before I read your reflections on John 3:16 I only believed God existed. But now you have me starting to believe that God actually cares for us. Thanks for all your words on the mystery of suffering and the purpose of prayer. There are no more questions, only a request, a big one. You know that I think with my heart more than with my head. Would you be willing to share how your brother Neil's suffering and death affected your personal life, how it touched the core of who you are? If you prefer not to fulfill this request because it would be too painful or inconvenient for you, please disregard

*my request, and don't feel guilty about not
enriching the sorry state of my spiritual life!*

Your friend...still!

Ellen

ELLEN, YOU ARE by no means the only one
nowadays who appreciates the value of well-
expressed insights into a particular topic yet who
waits for a writer or speaker to tell them their personal
experiences on the topic. You are more of an existential
phenomenologist than you realize! All I am saying is
that you have a preference for experience as a teacher
of the reality of life. Having given that preamble, the
answer is a definite yes; I will share what I learned
from my experience with Neil's suffering, especially as
it affected the core of my being.

The most intense and richly rewarding pastoral
ministry I ever experienced was being the chaplain at
St. Clare's Hospital in mid-town Manhattan during
the summer of 1963. There I anointed my first several
hundred persons with the Sacrament of the Sick. Most
passed from this life to eternity. At the time I thought
that I had a "black thumb," the opposite of a good
gardener's "green thumb."

While pain and suffering surrounded me and
filled up my senses at times, I confess now that this

suffering never touched my heart. Yes, I was genuinely concerned and sensitively compassionate to the patients and their survivors, yet I have to admit honestly that their pain was always *their* pain, their loss was always *their* loss. I was young and life held nothing I was afraid to tackle, no problems I was afraid to wrestle with and reflect upon, so innocent was I of pain. Looking back on those days, I realize that I never cried or hardly ever even shed a tear. I was the Lord's "cool" disciple who left his family, put his hand to the plow, and his heart in a case of ice! Dead to the world! I kept my feelings safely stored in an air-tight cedar closet in my heart.

In those days, we Franciscans spent years without visiting at length with our families at home. Our usual visits took place in our friaries on the third Sunday of the month and lasted a few hours. While we wrote letters (once a week, according to the rule) in which we expressed our love and affection, we hardly ever had opportunities to hug and kiss our loved ones. Gradually, the indoctrination set in, so that we were liberated from the felt need to see, hear, and touch our family and friends. I definitely arrived at the pathetic point that I was happy and excited about being home with my family, but felt no real sadness or loss or struggle to part company with them.

My priestly and religious formation and education gave me a head full of reflections on suffering and the mystery of evil and a heart that was wrapped with a protective insulation that prevented it from being touched and moved to tears. I was typical!

Conversion to Compassion

To experience many times daily the raw pain of my brother Neil as I changed the dressing on his left hip where once there was a leg, as I assisted him in bathing whether in a shower or with a wash-basin, in helping him dress, in handing him his crutches, brought on a massive meltdown of this iceberg. How it changed me! Pain is real and hurts real, beautiful, loving people. If I did not change—or, if God did not "save" me through Neil's suffering—how many "Titanics" would I have sunk by sheer massive iciness? "God Save the King" they sang as the historic Titanic went down; God saved this servant from being an insufferable menace through my experience of caring for Neil. His death gave me new life, and he continues to live in me whenever pain comes into my presence. Today, thank God, I am a world class crier with the capacity of an ocean of tears!

A relatively recent experience of listening to John Koch, a father of four, and dying of a brain cancer, had a profound effect on me. John's wife, Amy, had been in treatment following breast cancer seven months prior to John's diagnosis. Before John knew he had cancer, he prayed to God: Lord, if it is possible, let the cup of sorrow that Amy is drinking pass to me. His deep love for his "pert and perky" wife and his love and concern about the future welfare of his young family moved him to offer his life in exchange that she might be spared. A week after she received a good report from her doctor, John was diagnosed with cleoblastoma (in layperson's terms, a crab- or spider-like cancer that spreads its deadly claws or tentacles in all directions to make it impossible to remove). He died three months after being diagnosed and Amy is holding her own against the deadly disease.

What John Koch did reveals a great faith and an even larger heart. When Neil was going through his ordeal of suffering, could I and would I pray, "Lord, if it is possible, let this cross of Neil's pass to me." When I first heard that Neil had cancer, and if someone had asked then, I might have said, "Oh, why Neil? He's taking care of our invalid mother. Take me; my Province has lots of Friars to take my place." Yet, as the bad news of cancer turned into the horrible madness of amputation, I could not, nor did I dare, to ask to take his place. God forgive me for my dread of such pain. I didn't believe I could bear such suffering. I don't know how Neil did. All I know is that I could not choose it.

Of all the "proofs" of God's love for us, none convinces me more powerfully than that Jesus freely chose the Cross that we may live and have Life.

The Faith Challenge of Personal Suffering

In the years after Neil's death, I have realized that it is one thing to be able to ponder and discern eventually the workings of God's will in and through Neil's suffering and death, but, it would be an altogether different reality for me personally to be able to appreciate and appropriate God's will if such a cross were mine and not Neil's. While I learned what pain was like, I still was distant from the pain as my pain. To understand the meaning and value of suffering in Neil's or our Lord's life is still totally different from recognizing the meaning when the suffering and pain are mine.

Aside from a deviated septum, occasional bouts with allergies, a bone spur in my heel, and being overweight, I have not known any serious medical problems, thank God. Perhaps God, knowing what a coward I am with pain, has spared me. Perhaps, my time of poor health awaits me as I try to push back three score and ten years. It is a secret, known only to God, whether my faith in God and his caring presence is real when and if a painful sickness strikes me.

My faith in God's love derives from some personal encounters with God. During a month long retreat alone on a mountain outside Denver, I experienced God's powerful and purifying presence for several hours. My soul was entirely illuminated with a glaring, penetrating, and painful Light that exposed my sinful life for all its ugliness. After a period of sobbing and tears, an incredible joy began to suffuse my whole being. Coming down the mountain, I heard the Spirit whisper, "Daniel, you have come through this struggle. Rejoice, renew your commitment to living a life of concrete, small, humble acts of love." The next day my sister, Peggy, phoned to tell me to come home, "Neil needs you." For the next three months I committed myself to living a life of concrete, small, humble acts of love for my brother, my mother, and my family especially.

All of these things — my month-long retreat as I struggled with my vocation, my meeting in the Rocky Mountains with a forgiving, reconciling God, and the Spirit's message about humble service and Neil's need for me — are evidence for my belief in a God who cares, and who will care if ever the heavy cross of suffering is placed on my shoulder. I had several other experiences that were not as major as the one in Denver, yet they were unmistakably the doings of the Incomprehensible Mystery yet everywhere obvious. Again, whether my faith is real enough to sustain me in such a situation as afflicted Neil is a secret known only to God.

Painful and Humorous Remembrances

The prolific author, Anonymous, offers this sobering thought: When we stand before God on Judgment Day we will neither be asked about our accomplishments nor about our failed enterprises. We will be asked two questions: How have you loved? What wisdom have you learned?

The last six months of Neil's life contain some precious moments of love and learning that I shall never forget. Some were unbelievably painful, some unusually humorous.

Our Nearest Angels

There is no way in this world that Neil and Mom would have coped with the last months of Neil's life without God sending "angels" to minister to them. Mary and John Klein, our next-door neighbors, earned their wings by being attentive to the ordinary, every day needs of Neil and Mom. Besides food shopping, paying bills, servicing the car, mowing the lawn, fixing the refrigerator and hundreds of other tasks, they were a vaudeville team providing humor that probably did more good than any medicine. Long before Monica, Tess, and Andrew, the Lanahans were Touched by Angels!

Home Alone

Two weeks after his surgery, Neil with his crutches, and Mom with multiple sclerosis and her walker, were home alone one morning. Mom set out on a mission to turn off the light in the breeze-way between the kitchen and the garage. In reaching out for the light switch, Mom lost her balance and went tumbling down the two steps into the breeze-way uttering aloud the prayer, "Oh, my God...oh, my God, help me!"

After she landed and realized that she did not hit her head or suffer any injury, she called out for Neil to come. Meanwhile, Neil was two rooms away and heard her "disappear." Grabbing his crutches, he hobbled towards the kitchen and then heard her cries for help. When the handicapped son's eyes met the eyes of the embarrassed, uninjured mother lying on the breeze-way floor, they realized their complete mutual helplessness. What did they do? They started to smile and then to laugh until they almost wet their pants! Sometimes things get so bad that you either laugh or cry. There is not always a big difference between laughing and crying. Their sense of humor got them through until Neil called 911.

Joy to the World—Humbug!

One of the lowest moments of my life came at Christmas time 1973. My sister, Maureen (a.k.a. Sr. Genevieve), a Little Sister of the Poor, arrived home for a holiday visit only to find Neil in pain as the melanoma surfaced again, this time in the form of a lump on the right side of his head. Immediately, Maureen knew that Neil needed to be admitted to a hospital.

Like most people, Neil always enjoyed Christmas itself and derived deep satisfaction in giving wonderful gifts to all of us. With three siblings in religious life, Neil was the only wage earner and he was always most generous. However, his last Christmas on earth was not to be a happy one. Having researched melanoma for months, he knew that the lump meant his condition was terminal. His hope began to vanish. His face revealed no trace of it.

During this great season of joy, classes of students from nearby schools came to the hospital to lift the spirits of the sick by sharing their joy with Christmas carols. God bless them for their acts of charity! Certainly, those patients who were on the mend after successful surgery or medical services were happy to hear the kids. It was an entirely different experience for Neil and the other terminally ill patients.

The carolers would arrive around three o'clock to bring their joy to the world to Mountainside Hospital, Montclair, New Jersey. I cannot describe how awful it was to hear them coming down the corridor. I tried to shield Neil from them by closing the door. If I could have performed a miracle, I would have made Neil temporarily deaf! To this day, I shudder deep down inside whenever my mind flashes scenes from that nightmare. I cried all the way home and through the night. My mother did not need to ask how Neil was doing that day; she was our sorrowful mother, bearing Pieta-like the weight of her son's dying. It was the darkest night of six months of night.

Neil-sen Ratings

My sister Peggy (a.k.a. Sr. Jean Aquinas, O.P.) a Dominican Sister of Amityville, New York, came home every weekend during Neil's last six months.

She contributed an invaluable service of love in being present to Neil and Mom and in providing decent meals. Meals on Wheels came during the weekdays.

No one can put together a meal as fast as Peggy, Neil told me. Most days or evenings, he had a good appetite and appreciated her offerings. Peggy had helped cook meals when she was a teenager. But, since entering the convent, her culinary skills had been allowed to lay dormant. Therefore, it was expected that her weekends of cooking would be a learning experience for everyone. Peggy laughed when I told her that Neil had observed that there were never any leftovers.

Being a math teacher, Peggy knew how to add. So, if there were three people eating, you used three potatoes whether you baked or boiled and mashed them. You cooked three pieces of meat whether hotdogs, hamburgers, lamb or pork chops. Why would anyone need more than one? Gradually, Peggy provided for seconds on certain items. In an effort to express gratitude and encourage Peggy in her culinary accomplishments, there were the "Neil-sen" ratings: Peggy, that meal was a seven going on an eight. Only her eye-round roast made it to a perfect ten!

Tuesdays With Neil

Following the surgery and rehabilitation to the point that Neil was able to travel, we went three times a week to the Kessler Institute in West Orange, New Jersey, for therapy, measurings, and fittings for a leg prosthesis. While I knew, barring a miracle, that Neil would not live long enough to need a prosthesis, I realized also that we can never take away hope from a person. Those times of therapy and measuring were times of hope for Neil, and his spirits definitely improved during July and August. In fact, when the Director of the Kessler Institute, Dr. Carroll, expressed the opinion that Neil might possibly go into the permanent leg without the temporary one, Neil was delighted.

Someone wrote that a happy coincidence is God acting anonymously. While Neil was receiving therapy one afternoon at Kessler, I started up a conversation with a volunteer named Anne Friend. To our surprise, we had a connection. Her son and daughter were attending the same University at which I was teaching—St. Bonaventure in Allegany, New York. After telling Anne about Neil's surgery and my mother's MS, Anne asked if she could drop by to visit my mother and Neil, especially once I returned to school in September. Would you believe that Anne and her friend, Cathy Wolek, began visiting Neil and Mom every Tuesday night? Even after Neil died in January 1974, they continued to come to be with my mother every week for several years. Where was God when bad things happened to good people? God came "in person" in the persons of Anne Friend and Cathy Wolek.

Poets' Corner

There are three poems associated with Neil that I treasure. One, he wrote; another he read often, and one he never read because it was written by his secretary at the time of his burial.

Green Fields and Woody Places

The poem Neil wrote seems eerie to me. It speaks of the tragic sadness of war, which turns the apparently beautiful places radiant in the sunshine into the reality of graveyards for those who have "fallen asleep" in battle.

> *Green fields and woody places*
> *I see them all around*
> *I see them all around*
> *Green fields and woody places*

In sunlight they abound.
In sunlight they abound.

Green fields and woody places
Now so serene and bright
Now so serene and bright
Why so often the deathbed
And linen of warriors?
And linen of warriors?

Green fields and woody places
I see them all around
I see them all around
In sunlight they abound.
In sunlight they abound.

—C. T. Lanahan (1951, 1971)

O Captain, My Captain

Neil did not have many possessions. He lived rather simply and frugally. Though he did his studies in Economics at New York University, he owned very few books. A small collection of poetry containing William E. Henley's "Invictus" was always on his desk. He recited this poem to me on several occasions.

Today as I read it, I appreciate William Henley's profession of exaggerated freedom from all forces outside of himself, even his independence from God. Henley was a modern man come of age! However, I read it as an expression of Neil's firm belief in a God who has fashioned him in the image of Jesus and fortified him with a rock-like trust in the God who will not only help him through "the night that covers me" but who enables him "not to cry aloud." Like Job, Neil believed that nothing could conquer his faith in God. The Lord was the master of Neil's fate, the captain of his soul.

Out of the night that covers me,
Black as the Pit from pole to pole,
I thank whatever gods may be
For my unconquerable soul.

In the fell clutch of circumstance
I have not winced nor cried aloud.
Under the bludgeonings of chance
My head is bloody, but unbowed.

Beyond this place of wrath and tears
Looms but the horror of the shade,
And yet the menace of the years
Finds and shall find me unafraid.

It matters not how strait the gate,
How charged with punishments the scroll,
I am the master of my fate:
I am the captain of my soul.

The Quiet Man

The Watergate investigations occupied the major TV programming during the summer of 1973, and were my viewing fare whenever I left Neil's hospital room when he slept or the staff were ministering to him. In sharp contrast to the arrogance and condescension of a man who believed the American people were not entitled to the truth, Neil was our Honest Abe. His secretary at the Metropolitan Life Insurance company captured many facets of Neil's personality in a poem she composed at the time of his death.

Neil

I do not think that anywhere
There could be a person more sincere
Someone always there to give a helping hand
As was Mr. Cornelius T. Lanahan
He was always there to give advice
That you could trust to be precise

Neil never asked anyone for a favor
But to many of his friends he was a savior

Neil was a very quiet guy
And he was a little shy
But I could always make him smile
And forget his work for a little while

If I asked him for an explanation
Of a certain situation
He would take all the time he could
Until I fully understood

Neil gave every job he did his all
And he was always on the ball
No one else could be so enthusiastic
For Neil really loved the work he did

Neil was the greatest and I'm glad I met him
And I never will forget him
And I'm sure that goes for every woman and man
That had the pleasure of knowing Neil Lanahan
                              —Mercedes Gomez

Ellen, these are just some of the ways my brother
Neil's suffering and death touched upon my life. His

life has not ended, only changed. He continues to live in me and in all the people who had the privilege of knowing this gentle man. He will always be my big brother and a hero, and, as the song goes, the wind beneath my wings.

∾

❧ Conclusion:
The Mystery Continues

Dear Ellen,

Peace! As we come to the end of these reflections on your questions on the mystery of suffering and the effectiveness of prayer, we both realize that the mystery continues. In fact, as you and I examined various aspects of the questions, we usually ended up with more unanswered or unanswerable questions. It is now time (1) to make a good confession to you; (2) to make one last distinction; (3) to give a concluding statement. Thanks for your

letters, especially for the encouragement and confi-
dence they conveyed.

> *You are a blessing,*
> *Dan*

Confession

To be honest, I have avoided almost entirely the
question about why some people's prayers seem to be
answered, while others' are not. In the first chapter, I
touched upon the subject briefly. Some things we
must leave to the incomprehensibility of God's ways.
What we do know is that the last word has not been
spoken or written on the nature of the miracles in the
New Testament and those that take place in our time.
Did the curing power come from within Jesus and
within us, or, from outside directly from "above"? If it
comes from within us, we may some day partially
understand why some are cured and others are not.

We know also that some very holy people, Jesus
and St. Paul, prayed to be delivered from their crosses
and were not. Some people cured by Jesus neither met
him nor did they ask for a cure (e.g. the servant of a
centurion). While most of those cured possessed some
faith in Jesus, some had no faith. It is a puzzling
picture. We all know people who claim their prayers
are always answered positively. Such faith in God is to

be admired. Such people always have a strong prayer life and are aware of God's presence in their lives. They have confidence in God because they have detected God's hand at work frequently. If push came to shove, I think we would learn that their "prayers are always answered positively" means that God never abandons them or their loved ones when sickness or tragedy strike. Also, it is a fact that some go through life with few crosses.

Finally, I have difficulty with the promotion of the "prayer that never fails." If it means prayer never fails to help us, I could accept that conclusion. When there is the promise of a definite cure when a prayer is said for a certain number of days, we are into magic and disillusionment.

Curing and Healing

The distinction between healing and curing is crucially important. To cure means to take away or remove a condition such as leprosy or blindness and to restore the person to normal health. To heal means to take away spiritual blindness or remove an obstacle in our relationship with God. Jesus cured ten lepers, but only one was healed.

It is true that some people are cured but not healed, and some people are healed but not cured.

Jesus is the great healer of the people. He cured the people who came to him; he himself did not request the sick to come to him. The entire life of Jesus clearly portrays him as the healer or savior and not principally as the miracle worker of physical cures.

Jesus saves and heals us from the guilt of sin and from many fears and welcomes us into the reign of God's love. To quote again Paul Claudel, "Jesus did not come to remove suffering or to explain it away, but to fill it with his presence." Everyone who was cured by Jesus eventually became sick and died. No one gets out of this world alive! A cure is a good but time-bound blessing. Healing is forever.

Conclusion

Romano Guardini, a renowned theologian, expressed a wish on his death bed. When he came before his Judge, he wanted to be allowed to ask questions. He firmly hoped that God would not deny him a true answer to the question which no book, not even the Bible, no dogma and no teaching authority, no theodicy or theology, not even his own theology, had been able to answer: Why, God, the suffering of the innocent? (Karl Rahner, *Theological Investigations*, Vol. 18, pp. 207–208)

Let us imagine that God answered Romano Guardini with a series of questions. "Romano, would you have preferred that I never created the world?" Guardini's answer would have been a definite no. Then, God would have asked: "Would you have preferred that I created human beings without free will?" Again, Guardini would have responded no. Finally, God would have asked: "Would you have preferred that Jesus never became incarnate?" Guardini would have answered with a resounding no! Then, God would welcome Guardini into glory with the words: "Romano, let your mind be at rest. Suffering is not an intellectual problem with a rational answer. Suffering is a reality to be lived and understood only by those who embrace it."

While it might seem to be an avoidance of the question of God allowing people to suffer, it is absolutely necessary to realize that our task in life is not to find answers to mysteries, but to live the mystery by embracing it, by identifying ourselves with it, by journeying with it, and by being one with it. Suffering is not a divine puzzle to be solved, but a reality to be lived and valued only by those who embrace it.

Suffering is Not a Divine Puzzle to be Solved

Consider my brother Neil's suffering. We Lanahans could spend from here to eternity looking for the reasons why he suffered. Was he being punished for his sins? Was he suffering because he unwisely shied away from doctors and neglected an annual physical examination? Was his skin too fair for all the sun's rays it was exposed to during our vacations on the Jersey shore? Did the often unclear water in our hometown contain a cancerous element? If he had married, would a spouse have noticed the troublesome mole and saved his life? Was it God's will that Neil die young, so that he would not live a long, lonely life?

We did spend much time wondering why Neil suffered, but eventually we came to this realization: What difference really does it make to discover the reason why he suffered? The important and only concern is how Neil dealt with his suffering and death, and how present physically and emotionally we, his family and friends, were. Fortunately for the sufferer, the people who love them usually move beyond endless lamenting to being present and caring.

On the deepest and widest level, it is only the one who suffers who can appreciate its meaning and value. Whether the suffering is being borne directly by a person or experienced by another who cares for the person, the truth still holds. Only the ones going through the suffering and the ones walking beside them understand its meaning and value as "insiders."

The story of C. S. Lewis and his wife Joy's death from cancer illustrates the point well. Prior to his marriage to Joy, C. S. Lewis lectured often on the mystery of suffering quite objectively and brilliantly. After his beloved wife died of cancer, he initially could not speak of suffering without experiencing deep pain and wanting to scream. Eventually in *A Grief Observed*, he reflects profoundly on suffering as an "insider." Only the people who allow themselves to enter into the suffering understand. The mystery remains, but the meaning and value of suffering come only to those who make friends with suffering and death.

Another beautiful example and model for all of us was Cardinal Bernadin. His sharing about his suffering and his joyful acceptance of Sister Death taught all of us the meaning and value of suffering from the viewpoint of an "insider."

God the Insider

God never asks us to bear with anything that God would not also bear. When the rulers of this world, like the Roman emperors of old, achieved some great victory, they often celebrated it by erecting a grand monument to their glory. The people shared in the glory by shedding their blood and giving their lives to build the edifice. When God wanted the people to share divine glory, God shed the blood and gave the life in the person of Jesus. Jesus entered into our existence; God became an "insider." "Jesus, who knew no sin, became sin for us that we might share the gloriousness of God." (2 Cor. 5:21) The Lamb of God became the divine scapegoat to take away the sin of the world. Jesus did not take away the sin of the world by removing it from our existence, nor by explaining it away, but by accepting it and transforming it by his healing presence. What does this mean?

It means that Jesus took away the sin of the world not by removing it to some divine landfill in another world, but by a kind of "recycling." Jesus became sin for us, he absorbed all our sinfulness. He experienced all the pain of alienation from God ("God, why have you abandoned me?"). The nails of violence penetrated his innocent flesh as the crown of thorns mocked his claim as Prince of Peace. Jesus accepted all that the world of darkness had to offer him; he took it all into himself, then transformed it in the crucible of his sacred heart into saving grace. Jesus took in all our hatred, indifference, and bitterness and healed them before he gave them back as love, forgiveness, and compassion: "Father, forgive them, for they know not what they do."

Prayer of St. Francis

St. Francis of Assisi prayed for two special graces. Insofar as it is possible, he prayed, he wanted to experience the pain Jesus suffered on the Cross. Perhaps, the granting of the stigmata to Francis lets us know that his prayer was answered. In the second prayer, Francis asked to experience the depth of the compassionate love the crucified Jesus had for the world. Perhaps Francis did realize that love when he would tell the friars "Love is not loved." But, Francis definitely understood how Jesus took away the sin of the world, how Jesus accepted the evil that came his way and transformed it in the crucible of his heart before giving it back to us as healing, saving grace. It is contained in every line of his well-known prayer:

> *Lord, make me an instrument of your peace.*
> *Where there is hatred, let me bring your love;*
> *Where there is injury, pardon;*
> *Where there is doubt, faith;*
> *Where there is despair, hope;*
> *Where there is darkness, light;*
> *And where there is sadness, your joy.*

Grant that I may never seek
so much to be consoled, as to console
to be understood, as to understand
to be loved as to love with all my being.

For it is in pardoning that we are pardoned.
It is in giving selflessly that we receive,
and it is in dying
that we are born to eternal life.

As we conclude this book, it is clear to me that we are not saved by professing only with our lips our belief in the Incarnation of the Son of Man and in the Redemption by his death and resurrection. We are saved when we live life as Jesus lived it by accepting our existence as part of our poverty of spirit. We are saved when we enter into our sufferings and become one with the Crucified in his death and resurrection. Only the "insider" knows the meaning and value of suffering.

To live life as Jesus did means not to allow the things that happen to us to crush us. It is to accept with courage our sufferings and with God's grace to transform them into blessings.

To live life as Jesus did means to embrace our suffering and death by allowing them to transform and transport us into new life. Death is not the opposite of life for the Christian. It is the doorway to new and eternal Life.

There is no intellectual answer to the mystery of why innocent people suffer. Jesus is God's answer, for God hates to say No.

∾

❧ Afterword

Dear Reader,

Have you ever had an experience where you believed that God said no to your prayer and later found that the "no" was actually a blessing for you? Or have you ever received a no and realized later that some good came out of it for you? Have you come to understand the event as a natural consequence of a particular individual (such as the death of a loved one due to someone driving while intoxicated)? Have you been able to use that experience to grow or to turn it into a blessing by extending understanding and compassion to others going through similar experiences?

If you would like to share your positive experiences of graced moments following God's no, you are invited to submit any unpublished original stories to Daniel Lanahan, O.F.M., PO Box 40, Ho-Ho-Kus, NJ 07423. Once submitted, these stories will become the property of Franciscan Friars, for possible future publication.

Peace and all good to you!
Fr. Daniel Lanahan, O.F.M.

❦ *About the Author*

DANIEL LANAHAN, O.F.M., is the Director of the Franciscan Ministry of the Word team of Holy Name Province, New York. He has a doctorate in moral theology from the Alphonsian Institute in Rome and has taught for many years at Christ the King Seminary at St. Bonaventure University and in East Aurora, New York. Besides preaching parish missions and retreats, he is the Religious Assistant to eleven monasteries of Poor Clare Sisters. He resides at St. Anthony Friary, Ho-Ho-Kus, New Jersey.